D0069513

Ginny...
An American Toddler Doll
by
A. Glenn Mandeville

Published by  **HOBBY HOUSE PRESS, INC.**
Cumberland, Maryland 21502

Dedication

This book would not have been possible without the help of Ann Roberts Tardie. As an Associate Editor of *Doll Values Quarterly*, Ann has an incredible working knowledge of the *Ginny* doll market. As a collector, she has assembled a collection of Vogue dolls second to none. My heartfelt thanks go out this giving, generous person.

— A. Glenn Mandeville

Acknowledgments

A project of this scope could not be accomplished without the help of some very special people. My deepest thanks go to...Barbara Bell, Thea Crozier, Gary Fischer, Bob Gantz, Elaine Hydorn, Kathi Van Laar and Kevin Wedman.

ADDITIONAL COPIES AVAILABLE @ $9.95 FROM HOBBY HOUSE PRESS, INC. 900 FREDERICK STREET CUMBERLAND, MARYLAND 21502

© 1985 by A. Glenn Mandeville
Second Printing, August 1986   Third Printing, July 1987

All rights reserved. No part of this book may be reproduced or utilized in any form or by any means, electronic or mechanical, including photocopying, recording, or by any information storage and retrieval system, without the permission in writing from the publisher. Inquiries should be addressed to Hobby House Press, Inc., 900 Frederick Street, Cumberland, Maryland 21502.

Printed in the United States of America.

ISBN: 0-87588-266-8

Table of Contents

Why Collect Ginny Dolls

Time has a way of healing all wounds, or so they say...and time also has a way of making the insignificant ordinary playtoy a collector's item. So it is with *Ginny* dolls. Originally conceived and manufactured as a child's toy, *Ginny* right from the start took on a personality all her own. In the 1950s, considered by many to be the "Golden Years" of doll collecting, *Ginny* went unrecognizable as the symbol of liberation for an entire generation of women. It is only today, with our educated backward glances, that we see this doll for the brilliant statement that she makes.

Our society has not been kind to women who did not desire "traditional" roles, such as cook, cleaner, mother, and servant. This type of woman has been viewed, and especially in the 1950s, as "pushy," whereas a man having the same traits would be considered "aggressive." Play habits establish at an early age the roles that children will grow into. Perhaps Mrs. Graves herself, being an entrepreneur, and undoubtedly running into trouble in a male dominated profession, put her own subconscious desires into the personna of *Ginny*. Whatever the reason, *Ginny* became the liberating doll with the subtlist of messages...We girls are just as good as boys...we can do the same things equally well.... In the book, *Ginny's First Secret*, *Ginny* travels around the country on her own, fully able to take care of herself. This is not the central message, but is definitely the force behind the story. Never once is it questioned where the adult figure is in all her travels. It is spelled out quite clearly that *Ginny* is all alone. A mature, thinking woman-child on her own.

In *Ginny's* wardrobe, the same factors prevail. *Ginny* has outfits to be a cowgirl, an ice skater, a skier, a chef, and has a tailored wardrobe to indulge in riding, surfing, and tennis. What made this interesting from a psychological point of view is that through *Ginny* a child was not playing in the future as with high-heel teen dolls, but was playing right NOW...in the present. With *Ginny*, a child could achieve the courage and the *savoir-faire* to go out and DO...not just dream of a distant time when this MIGHT happen.

Interestingly, little boys were extremely attracted to *Ginny* dolls, which must have caused quite a fuss in the not-so-liberated Eisenhower years. Vogue Ginny Doll Fan Club Newsletters are full of letters from little boys who regarded *Ginny* as the same personal friend that little girls did. Why this cross over of traditional roles? Because *Ginny* and her adventures were EXCITING. And this excitement knew no gender. In fact, in retrospect, *Ginny's* adventures were in many ways similar to today's "action figures" for boys...toys in which boys can act out aggressive behavior. *Ginny* was designed to have fun with. Her very construction allowed her to be taken everyplace from the dirthill to the swimming hole; from the roller rink to the ski slopes. One cannot but think that boys must have been jealous of the relationship between *Ginny* and her little girl owner, and perhaps the more forward thinking parents of the time were not adverse to their little boy having a little friend. Who really should care if that little friend is a boy or girl, as long as a child can identify with the characteristics, i.e., the morality of the figure.

Today, with our understanding of human nature, it is easy to sit back and say that Mrs. Graves put much of her personality into *Ginny*. Perhaps even she was not aware that so much of herself and her own struggles against society were being revealed in the doll. But to children, unsure of themselves, the message was clear. If *Ginny* can do it and not be afraid...so can I.

The proverbial "boogie man" was put to rest when *Ginny* took that first step. A train trip, a day at Grandma's, a barbecue, all seem like nothing to adults, but to a child, these precious firsts are a challenge. *Ginny* dolls taught a child to take those first precious steps, and stand tall and proud. The little owner of *Ginny* could see that this little girl, 1/8th her size, could do it, and so could she. Add that to the virtually indestructible composition of the doll itself, and you can see that fears were laid to rest. Send *Ginny* up in a basket in a tree...she will make it back down. Take her swimming...she won't melt. All this added greatly to the self-confidence of a child.

Today, we as adults, reared in the heyday of *Ginny*, view her as a source of strength for our attitudes. One cannot underestimate the value and the lasting impact a doll like *Ginny* has on the life of a child. Be it a security blanket or a *Ginny* doll, everyone needs that crutch...that little quiet helper to take one foot and put it in front of the other, repeating over and over again, until one is walking...tall, straight, and proud...perhaps in some small way because of their favorite toy...their companion through many a year and many a crises...*GINNY*.

How To Collect Ginny Dolls

Collecting dolls is perhaps the most rewarding of the hobbies that border on "investments." With stocks, all one has to show for their money is a piece of paper. Should the investment fail, the ugly and unattractive piece of paper is rendered worthless, designated to the garbage pail...no esthetic message is stated; for all purposes you now have nothing at all.

With fine arts, such as country antiques, dolls, paintings, etc., should your investment potential fall through, you are still left with a beautiful object...an object that will add beauty and class to your surroundings. Who knows... perhaps another generation will find your taste worthy of collecting again, and re-create an investment potential. Dolls fall into this great category of "investments."

With *Ginny* dolls, one should avoid the so-called "middle market," i.e. dolls that are played with but original and commanding almost mint prices. It is this area that is NEVER a good investment. These dolls are for the person who does not know what a mint doll is, and settles for less, paying a premium price for imperfection. It is almost impossible to recoup your investment in a doll such as this. You would be smarter to do one of two things...buy a nude, played with doll, restore it yourself with original clothes, or pay a premium price for a premium doll. Both methods will net you a great doll of value, and one that will surely bring you happiness and financial return as the years go by.

Standards vary for collecting *Ginny* dolls from different years. The early bisque "Just Me" dolls and the composition dolls can be forgiven the sins of neglect...of wigs not tended to or of clothes improperly bleached. But the newer the doll, the more perfect it should be in order to bring "book" price. Collecting played with dolls IF the price is right can also be rewarding, as long as the seller AND the buyer realize that it is being purchased for pleasure, and not as a fine collectible.

In dolls, we really only have two classifictions. A doll is either perfect... perhaps old store stock, or bought for an older child and stashed away in a closet for twenty years, or it is an orphan, in need of a new wig, and lots of tender loving care. My advice is really simple...enjoy both types of dolls and love them both, only understand the difference. You are not buying fine art when you buy a played with doll; you are buying used childrens toys and they should be priced accordingly. One of the biggest mistakes made in dolls today is in the use of price guides. It CLEARLY states in the front of ALL price guides that the prices are based on MINT dolls, the dolls that are factory fresh, and perfect. Subtract one-half if that freshness is gone, and up to 70% if clothes are missing. The nude, wigless example is worth about 20% of book price. More mistakes are made in this area than in any other collecting field. Just ask a stamp collector how much a stamp is worth if it is cut in half! Ask an art dealer how much a slashed painting is worth; or a car dealer how much a car is worth without an engine. Yet in dolls, at every show, one can see HUNDREDS of dolls that are wrecks, clinging to the shadows of their former identities, priced in the mint range given in the leading price guide books. These dealers, at the end of the day after not having sold their wares, blame everything from the weather to the current President for their lack of sales, when the truth lies in the fact that they are NOT dealing in artistic collectibles, but in used children's toys.

Fortunately, *Ginny* dolls are one of the sturdiest dolls ever made. Virtually indestructible, they can go, like Corning Ware, from freezer to oven, and barely show a dent. The restoration of a *Ginny* doll (discussed in a later segment of this book) is a fairly simple thing to do. *Ginny* can be made whole again, without much professional guidance.

Certain issues of *Ginny* bring more than others. The gorgeous strung dolls of the early 1950s, before *Ginny* really had her identity, seem to be the most collectible, and with good reason. They are artistically and esthetically perfect. With their Nutex wigs, and delicate sleep eyes, they are the real treasures of the Vogue Doll Company. The next in desirability are the painted eye hard plastics, manufactured between 1948-50, followed by the molded-lash walkers of the 1955 period. People tend to want what they knew best as a child, and many of the Yuppies (Young Urban Professionals), long denied the pleasures of life on their road to the top, now are pursuing items from their childhood as their just reward for a job well done. It is this generation, the age group now in their thirties, that have the most disposable income...the money to indulge themselves on artificial suntans, french white wines, and dolls that they either had or didn't have as children.

Will this continue? Will each subsequent generation of collectors want to collect the nostalgia from THEIR generation? Only time will tell, but for now, today's collector of *Ginny* is sophisticated, liberated, and eager to acquire new acquisitions that will translate into the investment potential of tomorrow. Yet, if for some unknown reason the investment fails (a highly unlikely prospect), the worst that can happen is that today's collector will have a gorgeous collection of objects that deserve preservation. We collectors have an obligation to future generations that may not have the emphasis on money we have been forced to accept. It is to this future that *Ginny* belongs...and will always be a part of.

The Care (and repair!) of Ginny

Very few dolls were made as sturdy as the composition and hard plastic *Ginny* dolls. Designed to take years of hard play, these great dolls can easily be put back to their former selves with just a little care and common sense. As discussed in a previous chapter, a nude, played with doll is basically just a mannequin, and should be priced accordingly. However, if you see a little waif, with disheveled hair, and dirty face, it can be made almost mint, easily.

COMPOSITION DOLLS...While nothing satisfactory has been devised to repair composition dolls short of repainting (which is a mistake), these dolls from the 1930s and 1940s can be made to look better. Begin by restringing the doll properly. Doll supply companies sell rubber bands that are especially made for 8in (20.3cm) dolls and are very inexpensive. Using a stringing hook, start with the head, then pull the band through the body, hooking each leg onto the band. Finally, hook on each arm, making a loop inside the doll. These bands are better to use than elastic because the tension is already pre-set for this size doll. If metal hooks, usually embedded in the composition are missing, these can be replaced again from a good doll supply company. Usually a hook has just pulled out of its hole, and a new hook can be bonded with a strong metal glue into the original hole. Once the doll is restrung, she will begin to take on her former identity!

To clean a composition doll, I recommend a cleaner such as "409" or "Fantastic." One must work quickly, getting the composition clean with as little moisture as possible. Also, work carefully around facial features, using a cotton swab, as facial paint will wipe off along with the dirt. I DO NOT THINK ONE SHOULD EVER REPAINT A DOLL! It may be necessary, however to "touch-up" a missing eyeball, or whatever. Use a very fine brush and acrylic paints, and experiment on paper first before working on the doll. Usually just a touch of black in the eye will restore the "look" that may have peeled off. If splits in the composition are visible, fill them in with some plastic wood that you have tinted with acrylics, and learn to live with the doll's imperfections, rather than allowing someone to ruin the total historical value by performing a complete paint job.

The mohair wigs can be tricky, but I have learned a few "secrets" that may be helpful. Try to avoid washing the wig. These wigs are VERY delicate. The best thing is to sprinkle a little cornstarch in the wig, and using a dry toothbrush, brush it through the wig. You will be amazed at the results! To restore the curl, I suggest purchasing a small curling iron sold in dime stores that is made to do "tendrils" on people. This plug-in iron with a diameter of a pencil is invaluable for human and mohair wigs. NEVER use it on synthetics, as it will melt the hair. Use the pencil-like iron to shape tiny curls and bangs, using a photo of a mint doll for guidance. I can assure you, you will be thrilled with the results.

The clothing on dolls from the 1930s and 1940s was usually made of all natural fibers, such as cotton, and can be safely cleaned. I have tried a lot of methods, but the best seems to be to fill a flat dish with lukewarm water, add about 1/2 cup of a non-clorine bleach (Snowy, etc.), and let the dress soak for about 15 minutes or so. Remove, and let dry NATURALLY. NEVER put a delicate dress like this in the dryer. As the dress air-dries, it can be shaped, and by the time it is dry, will not need much ironing. If ironing is needed, use a cool iron, on the wrong side of the dress, and avoid at all costs that shiny "ironed" looked. Shoes can be wiped down with "Fantastic" also, and socks can be bleached in regular bleach. If all this scares you, buy some ruined doll clothes at a doll show and use them to experiment on until you get the feel of working with fabrics from this period. TAKE YOUR TIME...is the most important advice. I have a rule I always obey...NEVER RUN RIGHT HOME WITH A DOLL AND START "RESTORING." Live with the doll for a few days until the "newness" of your purchase wears off and you can see what you can live with in the way of damages. IT IS ALWAYS BETTER TO DO TOO LITTLE THAN TOO MUCH! Nothing is sadder than a composition doll repainted, rewigged, and redressed in polyester and lace! Your time will be wasted, because you have destroyed the identity. If a new wig is needed for a composition *Ginny*, buy an old mohair wig and cut it up to make a new wig. Usually just the crown will be all that is needed. If you sew, and want to copy an old dress, buy an old hankie or curtain from the period to use for your material. NEVER use new fabrics on an old doll.

HARD PLASTIC *GINNYS*...These dolls are MUCH easier to restore. The only problems encountered are "green eyebrows" on the strung dolls. This is a natural occurence when these dolls are exposed to strong sunlight. (Beware, it can happen to MIB dolls if exposed!) NEVER pay a "mint" price for a doll with green eyebrows. An advanced collector will not accept this flaw on a mint doll, and the doll should be priced accordingly if this has occurred.

The painted-eye hard plastics and the early sleep-eye non-walkers can be strung with the same looped band as the composition dolls, following the directions given earlier. Bodies and faces alike can be wiped down with "Fantastic"; face paint is not likely to come off, but don't scrub hard to be safe.

Wigs on the sleep-eye dolls are usually saran or "Nutex," a nylon base fiber. Both can be washed right on the doll, squeezing out excess water and applying a small bit of fabric softener as a "conditioner." Leave the doll face down for a few minutes to drain the water out of the eyes. A dry toothbrush works wonders to remove grime in the eyes, and untangle the hair. The hair can be set in *Ginny*'s famous "flip" by using three small rollers from the dime store. One roller on each side of her face, and one in the back, rolled up, and she is herself again. Put a strip of hairset tape around her head to hold her bangs down and shape the hair to the head.

The clothing from this period is usually cotton and can be laundered as described above — but watch out for taffeta! This shiny fabric cannot be washed successfully without losing sizing, which gives it the body it needs to hold its shape. Also, it cannot be ironed without leaving shiny marks. If your outfit is taffeta and soiled, fill a jar with some rubber cement thinner from an office supply house, and drop in the garment. Shake the jar vigorously for a few minutes and remove the item. It will start to dry before your eyes as the thinner evaporates. Shape the garment by pulling from the hem to the waist, and allow it to finish drying. You are basically "dry cleaning" the taffeta. You will not believe the difference.

Shoes made of plastic can be scrubbed with cleanser and a toothbrush. Socks can be bleached. If *Ginny* seems a bit pale, a little cream rouge on the end of your finger will restore her to perfection.

VINYL *GINNYS*...The dolls of the 1960s to the present can be cleaned with "Fantastic," and their rooted hair washed and set. As their clothes are made usually of todays "miracle" fibers, they can be soaked and dried and usually don't even look laundered. Don't, however, put them in the washer or dryer. The agitation is too much for a tiny garment.

Some collectors feel that this is the only way to buy a doll, that is one in need of "love." Many practiced restorers have spectacular collections they have paid nothing for because they have the patience to remove the sins of neglect. Others want only untouched dolls and are willing to pay for them. Whatever your choice, the rules are simple. NEVER pay more than HALF of book price for played with dolls. Analyze the work that needs to be done BEFORE you start, and proceed SLOWLY. DON'T "overdo" an old doll.

Finding and restoring *Ginny* or any other doll can be a rewarding experience. Who knows, even a new career as the owner of a "Doll Hospital" may come about because of your new found interest. Many hours of pleasure are yours as another part of the great hobby of doll collecting!

The Vogue Doll Story

Few people would consider the history of a doll company an intriguing story. Yet the Vogue doll story is just such a tale. It involves a woman determined to succeed in a business venture after the death of her husband, a society that frowned on ambitious women, and a doll that would prove to be one of the best loved toys of the century. The story would continue to spiral upwards until the 1960s, when a battle over television advertising would plummet Vogue dolls almost into obscurity, but like the phoenix to rise again, fall again, and then rise triumphantly back to power in the 1980s.

Jennie Adler was born in Somerville, Massachusetts, on May 14, 1890. Related to the Fuller Brush family, she was no stranger to creativity and retailing. At an early age she began designing outfits for family members and their dolls, and seemed to be a child for whom thought processes came easily. At age 15 her father died, and Jennie, like most young people of the period, was forced to put her dreams on hold in order to help support her family. After working at menial jobs, she landed a position in a lingerie shop in Boston. It was here that her first exposure to fine fabrics took place. After working there five years she resigned, and was married at age 21 to William H. Graves, on June 28, 1913. Three children later, and slightly bored, she began sewing and donating her work to charity. It turned out that her "friends" at the "charitable institutions" were selling her work, and Jennie soon learned that there was a market for her skills.

In 1922, she opened the Vogue Doll Shoppe. Her first attempts were to buy the German bisque dolls sold in chemises and dress them in spectacular styles. Her first achievements proved highly successful, and soon the entire neighborhood was disrupted by the traffic in and out of her shop. Forced to relocate elsewhere, she soon moved to Medford, Massachusetts. By 1951, two plants were in operation, one in Medford, and another in Malden, Massachusetts.

By the middle of the 1930s the name of the company was changed to Vogue Dolls. In 1939, Mrs. Graves husband died, and Jennie found herself the breadwinner of an entire household. One must remember this was in the middle of The Depression. It was hard enough for men to find work, let alone women. Women were brainwashed by society NOT to take jobs from men, who needed the income to support families. Mrs. Graves found herself twixt and tween...no one was coming across with aid for her family, yet an "ambitious" woman was not admired in American society. Determined not to let her family suffer, she expanded her business greatly, always finding time for her favorite hobby, collecting hats! Jennie Graves gave new meaning to the Easter Parade every Sunday as she exhibited the latest in millinery.

In 1952, small businesses were subjected to unfair taxation. Mrs. Graves made a pilgrimage to Washington, D.C., where she single-handedly persuaded the congressmen to reduce the excess profit pinch on small businesses. Her home town congressman remarked that Mrs. Graves had forever changed the way America would think about small businesses again.

In 1970, Jennie retired to Falmouth, Massachusetts, and continued active in many affairs of her company and the community. Mrs. Graves passed away in 1971 at the age of 81. Her story is one of a woman ahead of her time, faithful to the concept that hard work results in financial rewards, and a pioneer for the women's movement.

Without the help of the original "Ginny," Virginia Graves Carlson, daughter of Jennie Graves, born March 28, 1919, the Vogue Doll Company might not have been an American success story. In 1954, Virginia married Stanley G. Carlson of Brockton, Massachusetts, but stayed on as designer at Vogue. She alone was the motivating force behind the styles for all the Vogue Doll Family. For awhile, Vogue came out with over 100 new costumes a year for *Ginny*, all designed by Virginia. A brilliant designer, Ginny draped fabric over dolls until the right look was achieved. Like her mother, she was way ahead of her time, and was an outstanding leader in fashion design. In 1966, Virginia Graves Carlson retired to Falmouth, Massachusetts, to care for her mother, and remained active in community affairs and other interests.

Vogue Dolls was truly a phenomenon of 1950s ingenuity. While seeming like a big time operation on the surface, in its heyday, it employed 800 women sewing at home in what was another American phenomenon, the cottage industry. Cottage industries gave American women the opportunity to work within the confines of their homes, tending to their families and yet allowing them the flexibility to set their own hours. This is an important concept that history should not forget, as these women often were more productive than workers required to "put in hours" and stay beyond when the work was finished. The cottage industry concept greatly added to worker moral and incentive, and is definitely an idea worth pursuing today.

This introduction into the Vogue doll story will be carried out chapter by chapter as we explore the world of *Ginny*, and unfold her secrets one by one. Join us now on a journey to a kingdom, resplendent with a Coronation Queen, and learn about THE VOGUE DOLL STORY.

Vogue Clothing Labels

1930s. The writing is embroidered with gold thread on white and the tag is sewn folded in the outfit. This label was used on the "Just Me" dolls and on the very first composition dolls.

1945-46. The lettering is blue on white cotton. This label was used on composition dolls. It is folded in half and sewn into the outside back of the outfit.

Late 1940s. This tag has white letters on a blue "ink spot" background. The tag is white cotton. This tag was used on later compositions and the first hard plastics with painted eyes. It is sewn on the outside back of the outfit.

1950-51. This label is white rayon with blue lettering. It was used on painted eye hard plastics and the first sleep eyed hard plastics that have the earlier paler finish and mohair wigs.

1952-53. This label is white rayon ribbon with blue printing. It is mostly sewn inside the outfit but is occasionally found on the outside back of the outfit. It is used on the sleep eye strung dolls.

1953. White rayon ribbon tag with blue print. This tag is used on the later 1953 *Ginny*'s with dynel wigs. It is sewn inside the garment.

1954-56. This label is white rayon ribbon with black printing. It was used on the painted lash and molded lash walker dolls. It is sewn inside the outfit.

11

Vogue Dolls, Inc.	**1957-mid 1960s.** This label is white cotton with blue printing. It is sewn inside the outfit and was used on bent-knee walker dolls and the transitional doll with vinyl head and hard plastic body.
Vogue Doll Inc. MADE IN U.S.A.	**1966-early 1970s.** This label is white cotton with blue printing. This label was used on the all vinyl *Ginny's* made in the U.S.A. It was sewn in the inside back of the garment.
8 | MADE IN HONGKONG	**1972.** Label is paper with dark green printing. The number on the left varied. The label is sewn inside the garment and appeared on the Vogue *Ginny's* made in Hong Kong.
MADE IN HONG KONG 1	**1978.** White cloth label with black print. It was used on the Lesney *Ginny's* with sleep eyes.
D | MADE IN HONG KONG	**1978.** White paper label with red printing. This label was used on the Lesney painted eye *Ginny* from far-away lands.
MADE IN CHINA	**1981.** White ribbon label with black print. This was used on the painted eye SASSON *Ginny's*. It is sewn inside the garment.
Vogue dolls, INC. ©1984	**1984.** White ribbon label with black print. It is used on the new Vogue sleep eye *Ginny's*.

From the late 1940s to the late 1950s, there was considerable overlapping in the labels as old stock was used up by the home sewers. It is necessary to keep this in mind when trying to date a garment. Also, in the late 1940s it appears that no labels were used for a time. Instead, round gold stickers printed with "Vogue" were placed on the front of the outfit.

I...The Early Years

In 1922, when the Vogue Doll Shoppe opened, little did Mrs. Graves know that a huge demand existed for her work. Up until that time most dolls had been sold undressed, or dressed in just a chemise or simple outfit. In the 1880s, when the French Bebés were being imported into this country, fancy dresses and hats abounded from the latest Paris fashions. As the German doll makers began to force an end to the reign of the French dolls (through lower prices), quality suffered in the area of costuming.

Mrs. Graves believed that the clothing on a doll could really make a difference, and began designing clothes for bisque dolls which she imported. Eventually she turned to the "Just Me" dolls from Germany, manufactured by Armand Marseille. She used both the 8in (20.3cm) size, and the 10in (25.4cm) model, using poodle cut wigs and importing trunks which were used to create entire gift sets for the dolls. Today, we can identify these "Just Me" dolls as they are made of either fired bisque, or painted bisque, with fine sleep-eyes. Marked "Just Me/Registered/Germany" with various numbers, they are easy to verify. Some of the outfits from this late 1920s-early 1930s period have a small white cotton tag with "VOGUE" sewn in gold attached to the garment. The shoes are fine leatherette, and tie, with little pom-pons attached. Clothing styles are similar to those on the *Patsy* series by Effanbee, all of which mirrored childrens fashions of the period.

The collector of these early dolls will still be able to find examples in original clothes. They were almost too cute to play with, and many surface from time to time in flawless mint condition. It is not known with any certainty if names were assigned to any of the dolls, but it appears that the ones this author has examined that were still in the original boxes, did not. The boxes are plain cardboard, lined with paper doilies, and just marked "Made in Germany" on the end of the box.

1.

1. *Ginny*'s roots can be seen in this all original "Just Me," bought by Mrs. Graves and dressed at the Vogue Doll Shoppe. This example is completely original and is marked "Just Me/Registered Germany/A. 310/11/O.M." She stands 8in (20.3cm) tall and has a 5 piece jointed composition body with a fired bisque head, sleep-eyes, open crown, and a glued on curly wig. *Ann Tardie collection.*

13

As the situation worsened between the United States and Germany, it became increasingly more difficult to find these dolls to dress. Soon it became unpatriotic as well to buy German imports, and Mrs. Graves was faced with a new problem...where to find dolls to dress in her fabulous designs.

The appeal of the "Just Me" doll made Mrs. Graves try to find a sculptor and a company that could produce a similar doll in the new medium of doll making, composition. Soon Mrs. Graves' search led her to Bernard Lipfert, the leading sculptor of doll heads. Mr. Lipfert had done most of the *Patsy* heads for Effanbee, and Ideal had commissioned him for such dolls as *Shirley Temple*. Mr. Lipfert even copied his own dolls as can be seen in the similarities between *Patsyette* and the composition doll Vogue eventually marketed.

This end of the business was very new to Mrs. Graves. She had been used to simply ordering dolls and dressing them. Now she suddenly found herself in the position of making dolls as well. Soon, however, she was able to find a company willing to manufacture a composition doll, using her head, and meeting her specifications. Composition dolls, with their "Can't Break-em" advertising (first started by Horsman and Effanbee), had caught on very fast. For years, doll makers had had to listen to frantic screams from parents whose child had dropped a brand new doll minutes after it was given, smashed in a shower of broken porcelain. If you have ever dropped a tea-cup, you can identify with the way a porcelain object shatters. Dolls had become a "Sunday's only" kind of thing, with mothers allowing the child to "hold" the doll Sunday afternoons after church IF she had behaved, and not much playing with dolls was going on. Composition, made from glue, sawdust, and other odds and ends, then baked and painted, freed the doll makers and the parents from the fragility of playthings.

Ironically, as any collector knows, composition has turned out to be more susceptible than porcelain to the perils of "crazing" (surface lines in the paint) and outright cracking, resulting in unsightly breaks in the entire surface. Extremes in temperatures seem to

2.

2. Many elaborate wardrobe trunks were made for the "Sunshine Babies." This doll is 8in (20.3cm) tall and has curved baby legs. Her painted head is unusual, since most had wigs. She is marked "Vogue" on her head, "Doll Co" on her back. Her wardrobe consists of a tagged (gold sewn letters, VOGUE) bathrobe, and extra pieces of clothing and accessories. *Author's collection.*

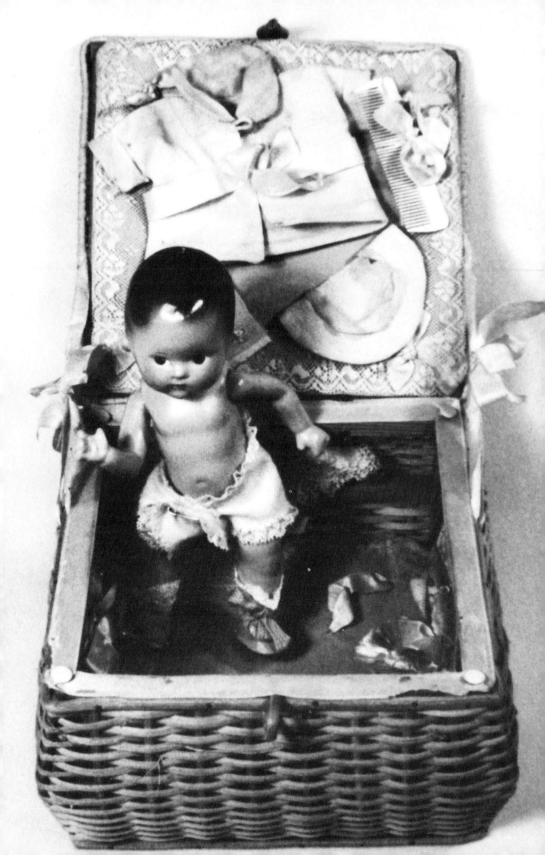

cause the most damage, as dolls stored in hot attics or damp basements seemed to have fared the worst. As a "natural" product, composition absorbs moisture from the air and expands, resulting in fine cracking in the painted surface which does NOT expand, and when subjected to extreme heat, dries out and splits open. Nonetheless, to a child who usually only required the doll to last a few years, this new medium was more than welcomed, and resulted in dolls being cheaper, sturdier, and more available.

Mrs. Graves became one of the first of the smaller manufacturers to use this new material to its best advantage. In 1937, all her dolls used this composition and continued to do so until 1947-48.

During this period Virginia Graves Carlson came to work for her mother, and eventually took over as chief designer. Like most companies, Vogue did not keep records of all their dolls for very long, never dreaming that someday they would be collected by adults who would want to know everything about how the dolls were made and sold.

New series such as the "Sunshine Babies" were tried, and had the same heads, torsos and arms, but were made with curved legs. Dressed elaborately, and often marketed in gift sets, they are as beautiful today as when made in the early 1940s.

For a time, when imports became tight, and manufacturing demands impossible, Mrs. Graves purchased dolls from the Arranbee Doll Company. These were marked "R&B" on the back. Later composition dolls were marked "Vogue" on the head, and "Doll Co" on the back. We will never know for sure exactly what existed during that time period, but most of the little girls were called *Toddles* and had this name stamped in ink on the bottom of her shoe. It seemed Mrs. Graves had shied away from naming her dolls, and resorted instead to series names, such as "Nursery Rhyme" dolls, "Fairy Tale" dolls, and "Far-Away Places." Very popular was the military group consisting of *Captain*, *Sailor*, *Uncle Sam*, *Aviator*, *Nurse* and *Soldier*. Also manufactured was a "Cinderella Group" with *Cinderella*, *Prince Charming*, and the *Fairy Godmother*. These characters, too, had their series name stamped in

3.

3. The "Nursery Rhyme Series" was very popular in the early 1940s. This lovely example of *Mistress Mary* is so marked in ink on her leatherette shoes. Her head is marked "Vogue," and her back says "Doll Co." The rich colors are still fresh after forty years. *Author's collection.*

ink on the bottom of their shoes. A later addition was the "Bridal Party," with *Bride, Bridesmaid, Groom,* and *Minister.*

By 1943 Vogue had taken as a slogan, "Fashion Leaders in Doll Society," and Vogue became incorporated in 1945. Separate clothing was also available for the little *Toddles* dolls. Exciting and imaginative accessories came along for the dolls — such as rakes, bars of soap, and towels. Through *Toddles* and the other characters, a child could at last have a sturdy companion. By the end of the 1940s, the best was yet to come, as manufacturing techniques were forever changed by one word...plastic!

4. A beautiful example of a mint-in-box doll, this *Fairy Godmother,* marked the same as *Mistress Mary,* also has her name on her shoes. Her original box adds a great deal to her value. *Author's collection.*

4.

The Accessories

5. *Ginny* apron set #7837. This was a cute set for "Mother and Ginny." *Ann Tardie collection.*

6. Assorted jewelry. Top is 1956 #6834, a pearl ensemble. Beneath is a charm bracelet, 1958 #3690, with heads of *Jill, Ginny,* and *Ginnette* in silver. ($2.00 from Filene's in Boston!) Bottom is *Ginny's* locket, 1955 #835. *Ann Tardie collection.*

7. 1958 *Ginny* separates. *Ann Tardie collection.*

N o doll in the 1950s had as many accessories as did *Ginny*. Everything from earmuffs to schoolbags was available for this little toddler doll. Stores carried racks of items, such as extra shoes, socks and eyeglasses. Separates, such as skirts, slacks and hats, were also sold. *Ginny* even had her own printed sheets long before designer linen was in "vogue."

To many collectors, the accessories are the fun part, as the dolls can often be found, but loose parts are a problem. Here is a sampling of some accessories available for *Ginny*!

5.

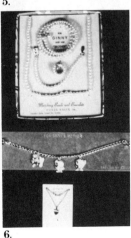

6.

7.

8. Left, 1957 #7912, "Dream Cozy Bed Set." Top right is 1955 #917 "Quilted Puff." Middle is "Beach Roll" 1958 #1560. (Has wooden pail that says "Ginny".) Bottom is outfit #7127, 1957. *Author's collection.*

9. From 1952...miniature suitcase #840, #837, dress set, and red velvet coat and hat. (Note box says "VOGUE" only, no mention yet of *Ginny* on boxed items.)

10. Various years mint-in-box clothing to show the boxes. *Author's collection.*

11. More of the gorgeous accessories available for *Ginny* during the Golden Era! *Author's collection.*

12. Everything could be purchased for *Ginny* separately in the heyday of the 1950s! *Ann Tardie collection.*

13. More and more accessories. The note paper came in a gift set with doll called "Party Package"...the red plaid items used a plaid that was *Ginny's* "signature."

8.

9.

10.

11.

12.

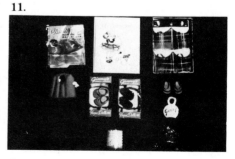

13.

II...Painted-Eye Hard Plastics, a new beginning (1948-50)

Towards the end of World War II, a new material had found its place in the American war effort. Developed primarily for use in creating lighter fighter planes, plastics soon began to revolutionize all industry. The doll makers, long plagued by the instability of composition, were ecstatic over this new development which forever loosened the hold composition dolls had on manufacturers. For ten years companies had experimented with formulas which wouldn't craze or peel, but the battle could not be won. As long as a natural wood base product was being used, the dampness and heat would expand and contract the material. Often entire shipments were returned during rainy spells, as horrified store employees opened boxes of brand new dolls, only to find them already peeling. Ideal seemed to be the most affected, and Effanbee being the best. Vogue dolls seem to develop fine line crazing, but many have survived in perfect condition for today's collectors.

With plastics, the main advantage was that new molds did not have to be made. Manufacturers were overjoyed because the quality of their dolls was going to go up, while the cost remained the same. Now dolls were washable! Wigs could be washed on a doll head, and no damage resulted. The new material was a dream come true for the doll industry. Many companies, like Madame Alexander, issued their 1948 line identical in every detail to the 1947 line, with one important difference...plastic. By 1949, virtually every manufacturer was using the plastic medium for their dolls, producing toys which today are virtually indestructible, and are truly the antiques of tomorrow.

Vogue began making adorable sets of twins, dressed in matching outfits as brother and sister, and issued an infant called a *Crib Crowd* baby, which even had rubber pants. For 1948, the company experimented with

14.

14, 15 & 16. In 1950 a series called "One Half Century Group," consisting of seven dolls, were available. Considered today to be among the rarest of all Vogue Dolls, they are all painted-eye hard plastics, except the "Miss 2000," which had sleep-eyes, to show the progress of the company. Shown here are *Miss 1910,* looking very much from the period, and *Miss 1920. Miss 2000* is costumed quite simply, yet conveys the message of a future time. *Barbara Bell collection.*

many new names and styles, including holiday specials and theme dolls. Nursery rhymes continued to be popular, and additional boxed outfits could transform each doll into a new plaything. These painted-eye hard plastic dolls are ALL marked "Vogue" on the head, and "Vogue Doll" on the body. IF A DOLL IS NOT MARKED, IT IS NOT A VOGUE DOLL FROM THIS PERIOD. These two years, 1948 and 1949, produced a great many treasures that have survived today. Just around the corner...transition, as Vogue discovered set-table wigs and sleepable eyes! The "Golden Era" of dolls, the 1950s, was about to begin!

17. The Brother-Sister theme is carried out in this lovely all original pair from 1948-50. Dressed in a peachy-pink color, even their socks match. Mohair wigs add the crowning glory to this great pair. *Barbara Bell collection.*

18. Another Brother-Sister set is done in tones of blue. Included with the dolls are these unique accessories consisting of an assortment of gardening tools, a wheelbarrow, and a watering can. *Ann Tardie collection.*

15.

17.

16.

18.

19.

20.

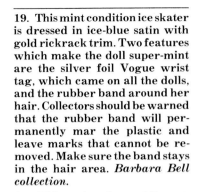

21.

19. This mint condition ice skater is dressed in ice-blue satin with gold rickrack trim. Two features which make the doll super-mint are the silver foil Vogue wrist tag, which came on all the dolls, and the rubber band around her hair. Collectors should be warned that the rubber band will permanently mar the plastic and leave marks that cannot be removed. Make sure the band stays in the hair area. *Barbara Bell collection.*

20. This painted-eye *Mistress Mary* is complete with her staff. Her side-parted mohair wig started a popular style that would be used on later dolls. *Barbara Bell collection.*

21. This clown is adorable in his taffeta clown suit and hat. The same basic doll as the Brother series, he shows the simple, yet effective costuming designed by Mrs. Graves and her daughter. *Ann Tardie collection.*

22. Perhaps one of the favorites of the storybook characters is this *Red Riding Hood*. She is store-mint in her satin cape. Her organdy flowered dress is labeled, and the basket IS original to the doll. This is one of the carry-over dolls from the composition era, as the author has one just like her in composition. *Ann Tardie collection.*

23. The "Far-Away Lands" series featured this Dutch boy and girl. One of the few couples, they were also made later on with the sleep-eyes. *Author's collection.*

24. One of the most collectible series from this period are the *Crib Crowd* babies. Basically the same doll as the rest, the only difference is her bent-leg baby styling. The clothing is usually labeled, and has a fine drawstring threaded through the neckline. Socks tied with ribbons and plastic "rubber" pants complete this baby outfit. Her chair is Vogue, but dates from the mid-1950s. *Author's collection.*

25. Every collector dreams of finding dolls still mint-in-box, such as this little girl. Her mohair wig is auburn, with a mint dress and hat in pink taffeta. Her labeled dress is cotton organdy, similar to *Red Riding Hood*. A perfect treasure in a Vogue box. *Ann Tardie collection.*

22.

23.

24.

25.

26.   27.

26. Representative of the little girl dolls of the period, this doll still has her original foil wrist tag. Her blue dress has an attached white organdy apron. All the dolls from this period had leatherette center snap shoes in various colors. *Ann Tardie collection.*

27. Perhaps two of the most exciting of the "Cinderella" group of 1950 are this *Prince Charming* and *Cinderella*. The *Prince* is carrying a satin pillow with a gold-tie shoe. His blue tights, blue satin jacket and hat add to his regal appearance. *Cinderella* sports a "jousting" style hat, and her organdy dress is caught up with blue flowers. *Author's collection.*

28. This little girl's dress, tagged and definitely original, is of a slightly different design than one usually finds. The bodice, short apron, and panties are of checked cotton, while the skirt is of taffeta. This would present a laundering problem as taffeta always looks "washed" no matter how careful the restorer is. Her hat is a combination of the two materials. *Barbara Bell collection.*

29. More *Crib Crowd* babies romping in the nursery. Even these dolls originally came with the silver foil wrist tags. These dolls have somewhat curly wigs, and are originally dressed in tagged outfits. The girl on the left wears a taffeta dress and hat in peach, while the little lady on the right sports a white organdy dress, tied at the neck. *Ann Tardie collection.*

28.

29.

30. These two little girls of the period are wearing similar styles in labeled clothing. The doll on the left is wearing a blue taffeta dress and matching panties, while the doll on the right is in pink cotton. Taffeta hair ribbons and leatherette center snap shoes in matching colors complete their ensembles. *Thea Crozier collection.*

31. Mrs. Graves love of fine millinery is really shown in the lovely hat on this doll. Her dress is of blue cotton, with white lace trim. The hat is a combination of the two fabrics, as were most of the hats of this period, and set off the doll's lovely coloring. *Author's collection.*

32. These two little girls ready for a party show so well the skill of the Vogue Doll Company. The doll on the left has unusually long braids, and is dressed in flowered cotton. The doll on the right is resplendent in red taffeta. (Note the tie leatherette shoes on the doll with braided hair. They were used on basic dolls for a short while. Most shoes are leatherette center snap. *Ann Tardie collection.*

30.

31.

32.

III...The Golden Years —
Experiments
and Triumphant Successes

33.

33. Transitional clothing and materials started off the 1950s. This Red Riding Hood has the same outfit as her earlier painted-eye sister. Her eyes are a delicate pastel color rather than the intense color used later on. *Author's collection.*

By 1950, Vogue Dolls, under the able direction of Mrs. Graves, had moved forward to become one of the leading companies producing 8in (20.3cm) dolls. Her success in making a little plastic toddler would soon influence even "big" names such as Madame Alexander, whose *Wendy* would compete against the Vogue *Ginny*, for the next 15 years.

The new plastic medium had lent itself well to being poured into the composition molds. Now, however, companies were discovering that more details could be achieved than previously thought. New wig materials spawned by the plastics industry were making innovative dreams come true, and even light weight plastic doll eyes were now available, replacing the heavy weighted glass ones, meaning that small dolls could now have the same features as their larger counterparts. Experimentation became the watchword of the 1950s. Plastics had opened the door for new designs; now it was up to clever people to translate these new ideas into exciting dolls.

In 1951, a new doll was available from Vogue. The same size as the painted-eye dolls, she had a new feature...a synthetic wig made of a new miracle fiber, trademarked "Nutex," that could be washed, set, and curled just like real hair. Mohair tended to be uncombable. Clumps of it would come out, leaving unsightly bald spots on the earlier dolls. With this new feature, the doll had more appeal. The hair could now be changed along with the clothes.

To introduce this feature, dolls were made wearing a plastic shoulder cape, just like a real beauty parlor, to protect her clothing, and came with a round plastic hat box made of acetate that contained little pink curlers. The other big feature of these new dolls was that their tiny eyes opened and closed, and looked as life-like as human eyes. Buyers were ecstatic.

This truly was a big breakthrough in doll manufacturing, and would set the trend for the next several years.

Mrs. Graves and daughter Virginia had avoided naming the little girl dolls of the late 1940s. Thinking that a child would like to name her own doll, they were identified on salesman's sheets with stock numbers and a brief description. For reasons still unclear, in 1951, that little toddler doll with wavable hair and sleep-eyes carried on her arm a card that said, "Hi, I Am Ginny." Not particularly anxious to promote this name, the salesman's order blanks from this period did not mention this name, but listed the same old stock number and description. Orders for the new dolls came pouring in, and written across the order blank was the name "Ginny." The public wanted this little girl to have an identity. Still not convinced this was the way to go, Mrs. Graves issued a series of little girls with names like *Carol, Lucy, Becky, Ginger* and others. For the next two years, the name "Ginny" was just one of many of the little girl dolls produced by Vogue.

To the people living in the early 1950s, creativity knew no bounds. Every industry was expanding, growing, and trying new things. At Vogue, the sleep-eyes had proved highly successful. Setable and combable wigs provided a child with hours of additional play value. Gradually other innovative ideas were tried; plastic eyes made of violet and odd shades of blue appeared. Soon manufacturers learned that even the plastic itself could be painted as was the composition and, for awhile, dolls were painted over with a bisque-like finish or a shiny wax-like coating.

By 1952, Mrs. Graves daughter, Virginia, had a daughter of her own. Nicknamed "Pixie," she had short, curly hair that was luxuriously thick. Virginia decided that this would make a great doll wig, and developed a way to make natural lambskin into wigs, utilizing the natural curly wave pattern to her advantage. Few people realize the impact that dolls have on society at large. The "Pixie" haircut, so popular in the 1950s, was actually named for Virginia's daughter. Mrs. Graves had, herself, changed an entire nation's business laws, and now Virginia's daughter had launched a revo-

34.

35.

34. A beautiful example of a transition doll, this one has the earlier mohair wig, and the delicate lip color of the 1951 dolls. Her eyes are the darker color used on 1952 dolls. Tied to her wrist is a heart, original, that says, "I Love You." *Barbara Bell collection.*

35. Very popular today are the pairs, such as this 1951 *Cowboy and Cowgirl.* His curly chaps and plaid shirt go well with his girlfriend. The mohair wigs date these dolls from 1951. The silver foil wrist tag is applicable for all the dolls. *Barbara Bell collection.*

lutionary hairstyle that would be refined all the way into 1962 on *Bubble-cut Barbie.*® This was the type of family that made the name "Vogue" a household word.

Even the *Crib-Crowd* babies of the 1948-50 period were improved upon. The new poodle-cut wigs replaced the semi-curly styles of the late 1940s, sleep-eyes added to the infant appeal of these dolls.

The real triumph of this period was the introduction of the *Coronation Queen.* Unsubstantiated rumors say only 25 of these dolls were made in 1953, yet this author has seen two versions of this doll (see illustrations). One is a strung doll in a very elaborate dress, the other a 1954 walker doll in the original store display box, with a simpler dress. Allowing for the cross-over of different models, it still seems that this doll must have been widely available as separate molds for the crown and scepter must have been costly to produce for only a very limited number of dolls. As a dealer on the East Coast, I can account for ten of the dolls, so it seems unrealistic to assume so few exist. It might be noted that the coronation of Queen Elizabeth II was one of the first televised historical events in this country. Viewers tend today to remember two events on early television. The coronation is one, followed by the birth of "Little Rickey" on "I Love Lucy," with Lucille Ball and Desi Arnaz. Interestingly, both events spawned massive doll campaigns, creating a market for celebrity dolls before the movement again caught hold in 1980, thanks to *W.C. Fields,* by Effanbee. (For more information, see *The Celebrity Doll Annual and Price Guide,* by John Axe and A. Glenn Mandeville, Hobby House Press, Inc.)

It seemed that the 1950s was off to a very good start, indeed!

36.

36. Another "carry-over" from the painted-eye period is *Mistress Mary.* She is all original, and her outfit is untagged. Many outfits from 1951-52 surface untagged. Perhaps the home sewers that year were not provided with as many tags as in previous years. *Author's collection.*

37. This Easter Bunny was a holiday special. His special hair is made of the same material as his suit. Collectors consider this a real find! *Ann Tardie collection.*

38. A rare version of a *Crib Crowd* baby is shown here. Her wig is the same as those used on the painted-eye dolls; her finish, however, and sleep-eyes date her from 1950. This proves over again that materials were used up as new issues came out. *Ann Tardie collection.*

37.

38.

39. By 1951, the *Crib Crowd* babies had wigs like those used on the "poodle-cut" dolls. Basically, this doll is different from a "poodle" just in the bent baby legs. *Ann Tardie collection.*

40. By 1952, the "poodle-cut" wigs were all the rage. Outfits can now be identified by stock numbers from salesmen's catalogs, making identification easier for today's collector. This doll is from the "Kindergarten Series" and is #30. *Ann Tardie collection.*

41. This adorable "poodle-cut" doll is dressed in the 1952 "Sports Series." It should be noted that in the company catalogs, any doll was shown to illustrate an outfit. The "poodle-cuts" came dressed not just in the outfits pictured, but in all styles illustrated. The same is true for side-parted wigs, and hair colors. Many of these dolls turn up in original boxes, labeled, such as this one, with hair styles and colors differing from the doll used as a mannequin in the catalog. *Author's collection.*

39.

40.

41.

42.

43.

42. The "poodle-cuts" were so versatile, they could pass as boys. This is a 1952 *Wee Willie Winkie* from "Frolicking Fables Series." *Ann Tardie collection.*

43. Another mystery for the collector is that the outfits shown in the catalogs were often produced in many colors. This is *Tiny Miss* #41 from 1952, in two colors, red and blue. Each has its own matching leatherette center snap shoes. *Author's collection.*

44. Here is the same doll in green, with a matching straw hat. The author has seen cases where sometimes the company used a big hairbow as in the previous illustration, in place of a hat. Either are correct on some early outfits. *Ann Tardie collection.*

44.

45.

47.

46.

45. A platinum-blonde "poodle-cut" in #26, "Kindergarten Series." This hair color seems the most difficult to find today. *Ann Tardie collection.*

46. In the early 1950s Vogue issued several holiday specials. This adorable girl is *Merry-Lee.* Complete with little bells tied to her red organdy dress, she is ready to ring in the new year! *Barbara Bell collection.*

47. This is the only example of this dress that has surfaced so far. Obviously made for Christmas, the little red trees on the skirt are topped with green stars. The pattern is reversed on alternating trees. Unidentified as to year. *Barbara Bell collection.*

48.

49.

48. Most unusual are these early 1950s dolls. Dressed in matching taffeta dresses trimmed with white eyelet, the unusual feature is that they each have braids pulled up on top on their heads and stapled through the head with the big bows. 1951. *Barbara Bell collection.*

49. These two gorgeous skiers (1953 on the left, 1950 on the right), show the great detail in costuming that Virginia and her mother were known for. The colors remain fresh and bright more than 20 years later. Note the side-parted hair and violet eyes on the transitional doll. *Barbara Bell collection.*

50. In 1953, Vogue issued the *Coronation Queen.* Made as a commemorative to Queen Elizabeth II of England, this is a strung doll, and has elaborate braid on the dress (see 1954 version in next chapter). *Ann Tardie collection.*

51. *Carol,* identified in company catalogs. #26 "Kindergarten Afternoon Series." These name dolls are very collectible as they date just before the name *Ginny* was assigned. *Ann Tardie collection.*

50.

51.

52.

52. A 1953 *Bridesmaid* #56, in light blue. *Thea Crozier collection.*

53. Considered by many to be non-existent, Vogue made a very few *Ginny* dolls in a black version. Like Madame Alexander and other companies, their marketing research indicated that dealers in some geographical locations would not stock black dolls, and many felt a market did not exist for them at all. This doll is solid black plastic — not just painted on the surface. #43 "Tiny Miss Series," 1952. *Ann Tardie collection.*

53.

54.

55.

54. Every collector dreams of finding a doll like *Cheryl*, #44, 1953, mint-in-box like this one. Vogue was now starting to use a box with a logo. *Ann Tardie collection.*

55. The big name change! "Ginny Series" was the title of this little velvet outfit. #81, 1952. *Ann Tardie collection.*

56. In 1952, this "Brother-Sister Series," #37-38, were just as popular as they were in 1948-50 with the painted-eye dolls. *Ann Tardie collection.*

56.

57.

57. This *Sister* needs her *Brother.* The dolls were sold separately and not as a set, resulting in many separated children. #34, 1952. *Author's collection.*

58. One of the harder to find series is the "Square Dancer Series." Made in 1952 only, the ones shown here are the boy, #54, and the girl #50. All dolls had a call card for a square dance tied on their wrist. (Note: These outfits, complete with call card, were sold separately. Dolls illustrated in the catalogs, are not necessarily the only way these were sold.) *Ann Tardie collection.*

59. The rest of the "Square Dancer Series," #51, 52, 53. Colorful costumes and great fabrics in natural fibers make these outfits look "country." *Ann Tardie collection.*

60. The name "Ginny" keeps appearing and disappearing until 1954. This is *Becky,* #62, one of the "Debutante Series" from 1953. Tied to her arm is a little acetate box of curlers and a styling cape. *Ann Tardie collection.*

58.

59.

60.

61.

61. "Kindergarten Afternoon" produced this lovely *Kay,* #23. (Hairstyles and colors may differ from catalogs on all strung dolls). *Ann Tardie collection.*

62. "Tiny Miss Series," #341, *June,* dressed in red and white plaid. *Ann Tardie collection.*

63. 1952 *Bridesmaid* from the Bridal Series." *Ann Tardie collection.*

64. 1952 *Tiny Miss,* #44, dressed in pink with straw hat. *Thea Crozier collection.*

62.

63.

64.

65. This little boy wears an outfit not shown in the catalogs. He may date from 1950, or could be as late as 1953. *Ann Tardie collection.*

66. The "Kindergarten Series" of 1952, #23, shown in red and blue versions. *Ann Tardie collection.*

67. 1952 *Tyrolean Boy.* His sister is out there someplace! Like the "Brother-Sister Series," these dolls were sold individually. *Ann Tardie collection.*

65.

66.

67.

68.

68. 1952 *Tiny Miss,* #42, in blue organdy, with daisy trimmed hat. *Thea Crozier collection.*

69. The *Rainbow* ballerina from 1953 is a very rare doll. Her dress is made up of different colored ribbons sewn together at top and bottom. *Thea Crozier collection.*

70. 1951-52 unidentified dresses, not shown in catalogs. In an interview, Virginia Graves Carlson said that Vogue made many store specials over the years. Perhaps these were made for a special store. *Thea Crozier collection.*

71. 1952 #32 "Kindergarten Series." Black velvet bows flocked on satin is a great touch. *Thea Crozier collection.*

69.

70.

71.

72.

72. 1952 "Kindergarten Series" #23 in red. *Author's collection.*

73. c.1952-53 "Bridal Series" *Bride* and *Groom*. A lovelier couple is not to be found! (Note: All the boy dolls can be identified by their "Dutch boy" hair style — bangs and a short bob. The boy dolls were sold separately also, in boxes marked "boy doll." *Author's collection.*

73.

74.

75.

75. 1952 "Frolicking Fables Series," "Holland Boy," and "Holland Girl." A gorgeous pair of early Vogue dolls. *Author's collection.*

76. 1952 "Kindergarten Series," #21. *Ann Tardie collection.*

77. 1952 *Tiny Miss* #43 in yellow organdy. *Thea Crozier collection.*

78. 1953 "Tiny Miss Series," *Beryl,* mint-in-box with wrist tag that says "HI, ...I'm Ginny." *Ann Tardie collection.*

76. 77. 78.

79. 1952 *Pamela* #60.

80. 1952 "Kindergarten Series" #31. (Note: This came, as did many of this series, with braids tied with matching bows, or with the "flip" hair style, with one big bow. Outfits sold separately came with the bow in the box. *Ann Tardie collection.*

81. 1952 "Fitted Wardrobe Chest" #822 complete except for a plastic shovel. These "gift sets" are almost impossible to find. *Ann Tardie collection.*

79.

80.   81.

82. 1952 *Mary Lamb* in ice-blue from the "Frolicking Fables Series." *Ann Tardie collection.*

83. 1951-52. Unidentified, but believed to be *Alice in Wonderland* although no verification of this exists at present. *Thea Crozier collection.*

84. 1953 *April, #24,* in multicolored polka dots. *Thea Crozier collection.*

83.

82.

84.

85. 1953 *Cathy*, #61. Mint-green color scheme. *Thea Crozier collection.*

86. 1951 *June*, #41, "Tiny Miss Series." Cloth daisies on the hat are a nice touch. *Thea Crozier collection.*

85.

86.

87. 1952, *Sister* of "Brother-Sister Series," #36, in red plaid, #34 in blue stripe. *Ann Tardie collection*.

88. 1953 "Twin Series" *Cowboy*, #37, *Cowgirl*, #38. These dolls have silk-screened rodeo scenes on felt costumes. Truly representative of the "Golden Age" of dolls. *Author's collection*.

89. 1952 "Hi...I'm Ginny" with her "E-Z-Do Wardrobe." The red plaid accessories would be a logo for *Ginny* later on. *Author's collection*.

87.

88.

89.

By 1954, every possible "theme" for *Ginny* had been devised and tried. "Frolicking Fables," "Square Dancer Series," "Kindergarten School Series," all gave Virginia a chance to use her vast knowledge of design and fabrics. Her ability was improving with each passing year. Labor was cheap, and help was qualified during this period. It was an era of a worker being proud of his work. The Protestant work ethic during the Eisenhower years taught that satisfaction should come from the job, not the salary. Workers in the garment district spilled into the doll industry, and many were proud to be working on fine garments no matter what the size. Problems such as illegal minorities, absenteeism, alcoholism and outrageous salaries that plague the doll industry today (and the garment industry as well), were virtually non-existent in the early 1950s. Vogue, Madame Alexander, Effanbee, all were putting out a product using Post-War technology. New materials such as plastics and synthetics for both clothing and wigs, as well as garments, were opening new doors for the toy business. Collectors of dolls of this century view the period 1947-59 as an era of quality that may never again be matched.

The larger dolls of the period were going through many transitions. A new material, "vinyl" (polyvinylchloride), developed to mold bottles out of plastic instead of glass for safety reasons, was adding a new dimension to doll making. It was soon determined that the new vinyl material could be soft to the touch, and resemble human skin. Companies such as Madame Alexander first used this material for doll arms. American Character's *Sweet Sue* dolls used a formula that was so life-like it was uncanny. As technology improved, new processes were developed for inserting hair into vinyl, creating a life-like head with "rooted" hair. This alone revolutionized the dolls of this period. Now any hairstyle was possible.

Vogue, however, did not want to change the format of *Ginny*. Billed as "Indestructible,"

90.

90. Silk-screened felt was a popular medium for Virginia Carlson. This little girl also has a "Talon" zipper in her outfit. Her dog "Sparky" is ready for a romp. Outfit #71, dog stock number is #831. *Ann Tardie collection.*

Mrs. Graves felt the new vinyl would absorb ink stains, dirt marks, and grease (time would prove her correct), more so than the hard plastic. The big selling point of *Ginny* was her ability to go everyplace with the child. Even if the wig was destroyed through a play period such as "barber shop," it could be easily replaced for a nominal fee. There was very little that could be done to destroy *Ginny*. If you cut the hair on a vinyl doll, that is it. But *Ginny* could be given a new "coiffure" in a few minutes. Most stains wiped off the hard material, and it could not be subjected to injuries such as clipped off fingers, like vinyl dolls.

Still, Mrs. Graves and Virginia worried that time would catch up with *Ginny*, and she needed another feature that would make her contemporary with larger dolls, without sacrificing the basic indestructibility of the product. The answer was to make *Ginny* "WALK." The big dolls of the period now had this feature in the form of one leg that automatically caught up to the other, as in taking a step, when the doll was led. Sometimes the head turned from side to side. This concept seemed perfect for a little doll like *Ginny*! Soon a mechanism was added to the doll to make her legs go from side to side while her head turned. This, of course, would mean wear and tear on her feet, so Virginia designed a pair of sturdy shoes for *Ginny* to wear, made of vinyl plastic with a little side strap and button that could easily be fastened. On the bottom of the shoes it said "Ginny." This was the perfect compromise to keep *Ginny* current. Now a child could walk *Ginny* on table tops, floors, and walls. Her footwear, not as delicate as the leatherette shoes were, could withstand the same punishment as the doll itself.

Collectors should be aware when trying to authenticate outfits and accessories that the 1954 catalog, obviously having to be prepared before the dolls were ready, shows strung non-walker dolls throughout. Even the cover doll, billed as a walker, could not be so from the angle of the head shown in the illustration. Also, the new plastic shoes were not ready in time for Toy Fair in February of that year, so the dolls shown were 1953 dolls wearing leatherette shoes. When the dolls reached the stores

91.

91. The rare black *Ginny* was also issued as a walker. Outfit is similar to #74, but the fabric is completely different. *Ann Tardie collection.*

92.

93.

92. New this year was the "My First Corsage Series." This is #60. The acetate box contains a small corsage. *Ann Tardie collection.*

93. *Party #74.* New for this series was a "Carry-All Box" that could become a clothes closet. *Author's collection.*

most, if not all, were walkers with plastic shoes. The extra outfits, arriving in the stores later in the year, almost all included the new plastic shoes. We must keep in mind that Vogue, like other companies, was making toys — not collectibles, and that old stock would be used up before new stock was introduced. Many hard feelings occur between the buyer and the seller of "transitional" dolls because these catalogs are used as a "Bible." They were strictly a means for the manufacturer to tell the retailer what was available. Today, while offering a great deal of information to the collector, they are also a source of frustration to the legitimate dealer/collector who has handled thousands of these dolls over the years and knows that many variations occurred.

1954 dolls are marked "GINNY" on the back along with "VOGUE DOLLS, INC. PAT. PENDING. MADE IN U.S.A." The eyelashes are still painted, and the plastic finish is the same, or similar, to earlier dolls. Later in the year, a shiny type of plastic was also used, and handling over the years has caused these dolls to shine more than they did originally.

This was a big year for accessories. *Ginny's* pup, "Sparky," was introduced (though unnamed except in a later storybook). He was made by Steiff, the foremost maker of plush animals, and has a Steiff button in his ear. Little did Mrs. Graves realize at the time that this pup would turn out to be a highly prized collectible because of the tie-in of the names VOGUE and STEIFF!

Also new this year was furniture, made of fine wood and painted pink. The red plaid used for *Ginny's* accessories would soon be her "designer" identity, and new "Series" groups, such as "Whiz Kids" and "My First Coursage Series," would help round out *Ginny's* versatility.

All in all, 1954 was a very exciting year for *Ginny*!

94.

95.

94. This trunk set contains a 1954 doll and was old stock. Her outfit is a 1955 model, but all the accessories date from 1954. This just adds to the collecting fun, if not taken too seriously. *Author's collection.*

95. Separate coats, such as this #282, were popular in 1954.

96.

96. An unidentified outfit for 1954, similar to *Ginger* of that same year. *Author's collection.*

97. 1954 *Fitted Wardrobe Trunk,* #826. This set contains a doll, rain slicker and sou' wester, boots, three dresses and panties, two straw hats, plastic cosmetic cape, curlers, playsuit, bathrobe, nightie, slippers, one pair extra shoes and socks and a toy. Complete. *Author's collection.*

98. 1954 *Bridesmaid #65. Thea Crozier collection.*

99. 1954, #22, mint in original "Carry-All Box." This is the ultimate way to find *Ginny* dolls! *Author's collection.*

100. "The Whiz Kids Group," #70. Capitalizing on a TV show called "The Quiz Kids," where precocious toddlers spoke their minds, Vogue and Madame Alexander issued dolls using a variation of that show's name. *Author's collection.*

97.

99.

98.

100.

101.

101. 1954 *Coronation Queen*, a walker, in her store display box. For this photo her cylinder plastic lid was removed. Note her dress does not have the brocade of the 1953 doll. Base is marked "Vogue" on the display. Bought in a department store in upstate New York. *Author's collection.*

102. 1954 beach outfit #48 with a rare *Ginny* accessory called "Freddie the Fish." He is inflatable vinyl and gaily painted. *Ann Tardie collection.*

102

103. *Davy Crockett.* Not shown in the catalog, *Davy* has many features including a "Frontier Scout" button, and a patch for the child to sew on his/her jacket. *Author's collection.*

104. The competition between The Alexander Doll Company and Vogue was always strong, resulting in many arguments over whose idea came first. The Vogue *Davy* with a real fur hat, button and patch, predates the Alexander-kin version from 1955 on the right with synthetic fur hat, by at least one year. Like today, companies tried to outdo each other on a similar theme. *Author's collection.*

105. 1954 *My Kinder Crowd* #26. The dressed doll boxes are wider than a basic doll box. Included was a catalog from that year, and a heart-shaped plastic stand was provided to the retailer, although many did not use them. *Author's collection.*

103.

104.

105.

106.

106. 1954 "My Tiny Miss Series," #42. The catalog shows leatherette shoes, yet this old store stock doll in original box, has plastic shoes. *Author's collection.*

107. *Ginny's* Pup, as he was sold mint-in-box. *Ann Tardie collection.*

108. 1954 *Ballerina* #45. Ballerinas are very popular with *Ginny* collectors. *Ann Tardie collection.*

107.

108.

109. *Ginny's* furniture was made of wood, and reportedly handmade in Maine. The *Trousseau Tree* in the center is the hardest accessory to find. *Ann Tardie collection.*

110. One of the most charming sets made for *Ginny* is this "Trip Mates" luggage set. From this year on. *Ginny* had a "designer luggage signature" with her own plaid design. *Author's collection.*

111. One of the most popular outfits is this sweater and shirt set with matching hat, embroidered with the name "Ginny" all over the sweater. This year (1954) it came in both pink and yellow. #30 in the catalog. *Ann Tardie collection.*

109.

110.

111.

V...1955-56 — Molded Lashes and Pretty Clothes!

112.

113.

112. Truly a dream come true, is this doll from 1955. Mint-in-box with her catalog, she is similar to outfit #24 of that year, except her lace trim is made of heart shaped lace. On her wrist is that plastic "I Love You" heart used on earlier dolls. Her box is marked "Valentine Girl," so one can only assume she was a special for Valentine's Day that year! *Author's collection.*

113. 1955 "Gift Set" #865 complete. This was purchased with other old stock and is complete. This doll has braids, the one in the catalog has "flip" style. Contents of the trunk are *Ginny* in ice skating outfit, zippered house coat, two piece pajamas, taffeta party dress with panties, ski outfit (including skis and poles), fur coat and beret, slippers with pompons, extra shoes and socks. *Author's collection.*

By 1955, *Ginny*'s identity as a household word had been pretty much established. So had Vogue's sales policy. Unlike Madame Alexander's *Wendy*, who was available only in "better" shops, *Ginny* could be found everyplace, from the finest department stores to the corner drug store. Mrs. Graves firmly believed that every child, not just the wealthy, should have access to *Ginny* dolls. Interestingly, this seems to be the policy of the current management of Vogue Dolls, Inc., who have a certain line for discount stores, and another for doll speciality shops.

Ginny has been called "the poor man's *Wendy*, but I don't think this title was deserved. Despite the wide ranges of clothing available for *Wendy* and *Alexander-kins*, Madame Alexander dolls have always, in my opinion, been "shelf" dolls. I remember vividly all my little girlfriends of the period playing with their *Ginny* dolls, while the Alexanders looked down from shelves on high. The price difference between *Wendy* and *Ginny* during this period was not substantial enough to justify the above mentioned label. It really was just a matter of "image." *Ginny* had an "action" image that *Wendy* simply lacked.

Mrs. Graves and Virginia knew that keeping *Ginny* current would insure new customers, and repeat customers as well. By having the same size doll each year, one ran the risk of owners of *Ginny* simply buying new clothing for their old dolls. To avoid this obvious pitfall, two things were added in 1955.

The walker mechanism was kept intact from 1954, only now the body was marked with a patent number (2687594). The new innovation of 1955 was molded eyelashes. Gone were the delicate painted-on lashes of previous years. *Ginny* now had a rigid strip of plastic attached to each eye that made her even more durable and washable. *Ginny*'s furniture line was expanded to a very clever gym set, which obviously had to have many children to play on it, resulting in children wanting more *Ginny* dolls. *Ginnette*, the little vinyl sister of *Ginny*, was added to the line. *Ginnette*, the first all vinyl doll of the Vogue doll family, could wear splendid clothing that was a miniature version of *Ginny's* lovely outfits. Interestingly, *Ginnette* was not in proportion to *Ginny*, and looks like a science-fiction baby when placed next to *Ginny*. Children didn't seem to mind, however, and *Ginnette* became a huge success.

The "Series" names were dropped, and new titles such as "Bon-Bons," "Merry Moppets," and "Ginny Gym Kids" were added. The extra accessories offered that year were staggering. Jewelry, eyeglasses, roller and ice skates, curlers, boxed shoes and socks, notepaper — *Ginny* had more accessories than any doll in history! Virginia Carlson put together a budget line of fashions while expanding *Ginny's* fabulous wardrobe to deluxe proportions. Best of all were the fitted wardrobe chests, including dolls and clothing.

To those of us who were children in 1955, *Ginny* was a daily object in our lives. Stores, newspapers, and magazines were filled with either the dolls themselves or mentions of them. The name "Ginny" was one that would not soon be forgotten.

In 1956, The Ginny Doll Club was started for little children to correspond with *Ginny* and other *Ginny* doll collectors. It is obvious from reading these early letters that more little boys had *Ginny* dolls than one would care to admit to! Let's face it...*Ginny* was exciting, and "masculine" in the same sense that *GI-Joe* turned out to be. Little boys found the cowboy *Ginny* and the other dolls of the line to be as comforting as did little girls. *Ginny* was once again living up to Mrs. Graves personal crusade for liberation from sterotypes.

By the end of 1956, *Ginnette* also had moving eyes, and *Ginny* had a huge cardboard doll house and dog house for "Sparky." The Vogue doll era was in full swing!

114.

114. 1955 #23. New this year was a circular wrist tag with "HI, I'M GINNY" on one side, and the stock number on the other. This year, most stock numbers for outfits had only a "1" in front of the dressed doll number. *Author's collection.*

115.

116.

117.

118.

115. A favorite of many collectors is the "Bon-Bons" group of 1955. These dolls came with fancy flocked outfits, and a parasol that worked! These dolls are wearing #80 and #84. The buttons show *Ginny's* profile and say "Hi I'm Ginny" and were a premium when you joined the Ginny Doll Club. *Author's collection.*

116. A 1955 *Ginny* #36 and her maid from a later year arrive home from a trip. Various furniture and accessories available now gave *Ginny* imaginative play value. *Ginny's* "Mouseketeer" ears are borrowed from her "cousin" *Ginger,* another doll of the period made by Cosmopolitan Doll Co. *Author's collection.*

117. 1955 #47 roller skater. Virginia Graves Carlson displays her talents in design with imaginative creations. *Author's collection.*

118. 1955 #46. This year Mrs. Carlson redesigned the Dutch costume and made a short dress. *Thea Crozier collection.*

119. 1955 #65 formals. These lovely formals came in several colors. The only problem is that the material used is velvet bonded to a strange backing, and the velvet on almost all of these dolls, even when mint-in-box cracked. *Ann Tardie collection.*

120. 1955 #184, extra fur coats made of real rabbit fur. These were available in pink, white, and blue. *Ann Tardie collection.*

119.

120.

121. 1955 #62. *Ginny* had luxurious sleepwear, such as this peignoir of flocked organdy with a plain nightie. *Ann Tardie collection.*

122. 1955 #64. *Ginny* as a bride. Interestingly, bride dresses for *Barbie,*® by Mattel, have always been a big seller. With *Ginny*, however, the idea of a toddler bride is a bit bizarre. These outfits were merely issued for fantasy play, and were never publicized the way *Ginny's* other adventure outfits were. *Ann Tardie collection.*

122.

123. 1955 #56. Turquoise and gold outfit with gold slippers. *Ann Tardie collection.*

124. 1955 #61. A stunning check suit for travel! *Ann Tardie collection.*

125. 1956 #6402 on the left in yellow, and #43, 1955, on the right. *Ann Tardie collection.*

123.

124.

78

126.

126. A perfectly mint-in-box 1955 #26 *Ginny.* Some old store stock from this period has survived and has found its way into collections. *Author's collection.*

127. 1956 *Ballerina,* #6045. The *Ginny* "Ballerina Series" has always been popular with both children and collectors. *Ann Tardie collection.*

128. 1956 *Brownie,* #6052. What little girl of 1956 didn't belong to the Brownies. Many a little girl dragged *Ginny* to her meetings that year, I am sure! *Ann Tardie ollection.*

127.

128.

129. 1956 *Roller Skater,* and *Ice Skater* (#6047-6050). Again, Virginia Carlson shows her incredible design talents in these two lovely dolls. *Ann Tardie collection.*

130. 1956 #6064. This very unusual dress is made of organdy, with slices of crayon melted into the fabric. Very desirable formal from this period. *Author's collection.*

131. 1956 *Nun,* #6065. Most children, regardless of their religion, fantasize about being a nun at some point in time. Who knows how many lives were changed by this doll. (Her hair is very short under her habit, and this outfit was sold separately.) *Author's collection.*

130.

129.

131.

132.

133. 1956 #6043, 1955 #55. *Thea Crozier collection.*

134. 1956 #6065. *Ann Tardie collection.*

133.

134.

135.

136.

137.

135. 1956 #6028. Mint, in original box, with $3.98 price tag! (*Wendy* by Madame Alexander was $4.98 that same year.) *Ann Tardie collection.*

136. A group of late 1950s dolls in the "Hospital." *Ginnys* lent themselves to every play situation imaginable. *Author's collection.*

137. 1956 *Clown,* #6041. One of the most sought after dolls of this year, this outfit came either on a dressed doll or separately. All the dolls this author has examined have had braids, with one pink ribbon tie, and one blue ribbon tie, and leatherette tie shoes. The pompon slippers often seen on this doll are separate bedroom slippers. *Author's collection.*

By 1957, the name *Ginny* was known to virtually every child in America. Now the best selling doll of its kind in this country, Vogue was expanding its family.

Big sister *Jill*, a 10in (25.4cm) high-heel teen doll, was introduced. *Jill* was truly an innovation and years before her time. Her face was *Ginny*'s face, slightly grown up, with the same chubby cheeks and sleep-eyes used for *Ginny* dolls. Her hair was in a ponytail or flip style and, like *Ginny*, replacement wigs were available. She had bending knees, and gorgeous clothes, most of which were "big sister" versions of *Ginny*'s lovely clothing. Virginia Carlson dressed *Jill* in the real life fashions of the period. America was having a love affair with high fashion, and would until the "Hippie" movement of the mid-1960s put everyone in "jeans" for the next 15 years! Clothes were popular, as was looking pretty. The "Natalie Wood" image was a role model for little girls, and Mrs. Graves, still concerned that the public would outgrow *Ginny*, felt *Jill* would be the perfect answer to playing in the future as well as the present. For several years, *Jill* dominated the teen-doll market, despite challenges by Ideal's *Little Miss Revlon*, and a host of others. It wasn't until 1962 that a new star, named *Barbie®* extinguished the flame of *Ginny*'s success of the past 30 years!

Again, Mrs. Graves tried to keep *Ginny* current. A new feature, bending knees, gave *Ginny* even more play value, and like the features that came before, it was done in a way that would not make the doll more fragile, just more versatile. Virginia Carlson designed over 62 new outfits for *Ginny* in that year alone, and formals, long a staple of the 1955-56 lines, were carried over and redesigned with styling details even real garments lacked. Collectors refer to the 1957 formals as the best of all the Vogue doll clothing.

The dolls themselves, however, were being manufactured out of a new plastic, and did not look as life-like as the earlier models. Also, the

138.

138. 1957 #7091, *Communion.* **Another of the outfits highlighting special events in a little girl's life is this lovely lacey communion dress. The locket says "Ginny" on it and is a very rare accessory.** *Author's collection.*

walking mechanism, along with the bending knees, gave the doll a "stiff" look. Wigs were not as elaborate either, and have not held up as well as earlier ones.

Other new ideas in 1957 included a "Party Package" which highlighted *Ginny* and extra clothes, and an apron set for *Ginny* and her little mother. Also new that year were "Knit Kits," so a child could hand knit clothes for *Ginny*, an idea that Mattel would use years later for *Barbie*.

The end of the 1950s did not see as many notable changes for *Ginny* as had previous years. There are many theories about this, but my opinion is that Mrs. Graves, advancing in years, was aggressive long before her time, but not aggressive enough to compete in the "dog eat dog" world the toy industry had become. Always a lady, Mrs. Graves did what she had to do, namely go into business in 1922, to save her family. She was alone in a male dominated business world, and manners had counted for a lot in the 1930s and 1940s. However, like Joan Crawford, the same "tricks" that worked then did not work now. The late 1950s saw a new element arrive in the toy business now that American prosperity was at hand. This new element was not in love with the product, as Mrs. Graves was, they were in love with the profit. This new breed was interested in money before quality, and family name meant nothing, as these people would go into a new venture, milk it for all it was worth, then move on. Mrs. Graves, coming basically from a Victorian era, was committed to quality and providing children with a lasting example they could learn from. It was just possible that Vogue's ideas were outdated in the fast moving late 1950s-early 1960s.

Also, one must remember that Virginia Graves Carlson, Jennie Graves' daughter, was undoubtedly first and foremost an artist. In all probability, her love was designing, not merchandising, and as her mother became unable to assume the leadership of Vogue, it is doubtful that Virginia, like most artists, wanted to run the company the way it had to be run to survive. Anyway, since company records are long gone, we will never know for sure exactly what led to the decline of quality, and Vogue in

139.

139. 1957 #7073. Possibly the loveliest of all the formals, this creation features gloves on a white fur purse, and a velvet and taffeta gown. *Author's collection.*

general, but one thing is sure...*Ginny* was a 1950s phenomenon, but would be around until 1969 in one form or another.

In 1958, the Vogue doll family included *Jill* and her girlfriend *Jan*, also the same size, but with a vinyl head and rooted hair. New this year were *Jimmy*, a little brother for *Ginnette*, and *Jeff*, slightly bigger than *Jill* and *Jan*. The wardrobes for all these dolls are outstanding, and I have seen one collection consisting of all the matching outfits that ran through the entire family such as an aqua ski set that was made for all the family members.

140. 1957 #7063. This stunning pink formal was one of several of the gorgeous designs of Virginia Graves Carlson. *Ann Tardie collection.*

141. 1957 #7075. Although not billed as a Christmas outfit, this incredible red velvet formal is a holiday treasure. *Author's collection.*

140.

141.

By 1959, some of the old series had been revived and updated, including "Far-Away Lands," and some four dozen new outfits. Also new were patterns for *Ginny* and little girls. With these patterns, a skilled home sewer could make matching outfits for *Ginny* and her little mother. In my opinion, much of the "pizaaz" was gone from *Ginny*, and the emphasis on "cuteness" was being overdone. Little boys seemed to have lost interest in *Ginny*, as her new "Sunday School" image was not exciting enough for them. Her new outfits consisted of clothing designed to follow through a little girl's day, from pajamas to school dresses, and play clothes, back to pajamas. Pretty ordinary and pretty boring! Imaginative accessories such as jewelry for *Ginny* and her little mother were carrying the line, but clearly the emphasis was on *Ginny* needing "mothering" rather than a friend. This factor was inconsistent to the earlier philosophy of Vogue, as it would seem that pre-teen girls wanted less mothering and more glamor as they approached a time in their lives that increasingly, each decade, held more glitter than the generation before. "Teendom" beckoned on the horizon like a lighthouse in the fog. Adding to the downfall of *Ginny* was the fact that Mrs. Graves and Virginia were making *Ginny* more and more "dependent" on a little mother, when those little mothers were trying to be more independent, and live the life shown them every week on "The Donna Reed Show" and "Father Knows Best." It was this adolescent world of beach parties and proms, joy rides and soda shops, that glittered on the edge of a young girl's life in 1959. There was increasingly less and less of a place for *Ginny*.

Many, however, would never care to forget growing up in the 1950s, and having *Ginny* be a part of their lives.

142.

142. 1957 #7042. Frilly hats were quite common with these outfits. *Thea Crozier collection.*

143. 1957 #7040. *Ginny* and *Sparky* stand in front of the book, *Ginny's First Secret.* Authored by Lee Kingman, and published by Phillips Publishers, this book's "secret" is secondary to the message of *Ginny's* independence as a traveler. (By the way, her "secret" is..."Open your heart - Open your mind - Look for the best. And that's what you'll find!") *Author's collection.*

144. *Ginny* and *Jill* go skiing! These matching outfits exemplify the wide range of matching costumes available for *Jill* and *Ginny.*

143.

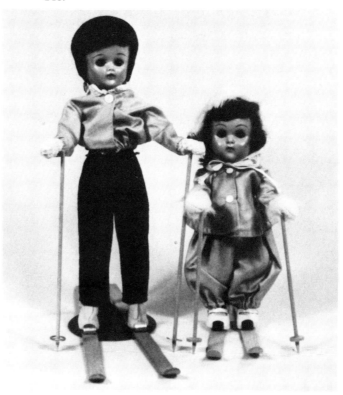

144.

145. The "Ginny Gym Set," sur-
rounded by various years' *Ginnys,*
and *Jills.* The play value of a set
like this is extraordinary! *Author's
collection.*

146. 1957 #7060. The cover outfit
for the 1957 catalog, this pink
velveteen costume came in a
matching version for *Jill* and
Ginnette. Author's collection.

145.

146.

147.

148.

147. 1957 #7865. This untouched old stock gift set complete with cardboard overliner, is a collectors treasure! The "Fitted Vacation Trunk" includes a doll in basic panties, dressed in nightie and robe in waffle piqué, and a cowgirl outfit, a houndstooth check school dress, raincoat, hat, and a formal. Its original price is a stomach-turning — $15! *Ann Tardie collection.*

148. 1957 #7866. "Fitted Trousseau Chest." This gorgeous pink wooden box features trays that swing out and include *Ginny* in bride outfit, five additional outfits, fur coat, raincoat, umbrella, and many accessories. It's original price was $29.95. The box could be used for a jewelry box later on. It is almost impossible to even place a value today on such a find! *Ann Tardie collection.*

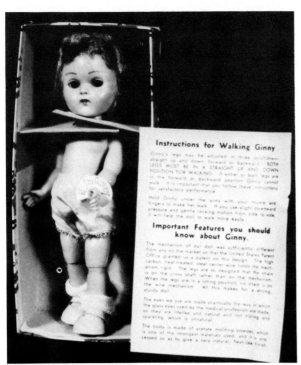

149

149. 1957 #7109, basic doll. Box is marked "Auburn Ponytail/ Undressed Ginny/$2.00." *Ann Tardie collection.*

150. 1957 #7044 in yellow, and #7055, pink. *Ann Tardie collection.*

150.

151. 1957 #7182, raincoat (available only as a boxed outfit), and #7053 in gorgeous pink felt. *Ann Tardie collection.*

152. 1958 #1162. An adorable party dress from this period. *Ann Tardie collection.*

153. 1959 #1259, *Hawaiian.* This fabulous outfit would later be copied by other companies, but the wonderful wooden surf board would belong only to *Ginny! Ann Tardie collection.*

151.

152.

153.

154.

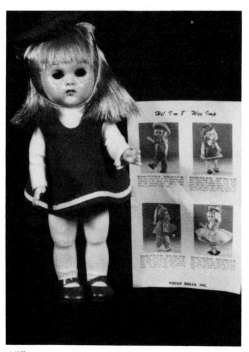

155.

154. 1959 #1256 *British Islander*. The "Far-Away Lands Series" carried *Ginny* into the 1970s! *Ann Tardie collection.*

155. 1960 #9131 *Wee Imp*. This friend of *Ginny's* had straight red hair, green eyes, and freckles. She was referred to as "mischievous." Madame Alexander also had a similar doll this year called *Maggie-Mix-up,* with identical coloring and personality to be *Wendy's* friend. (Note: The *Wee Imp* had four outfits all her own, but are tagged the same as *Ginny's.*) *Ann Tardie collection.*

By the 1960s, Saturday morning had become a big event in the life of a child. After a hectic week at school, children felt that this was their time. Shows such as "Sky King" and "Fury" were adventure stories aimed at children's imaginations. The image of *Ginny* as an adventuresome toddler would have fit perfectly into this time frame, however, as previously discussed, Vogue had taken a different path, making *Ginny* into a demure, sweet child — not exactly a Saturday morning heroine like the young girl "Penny" on "Sky King."

Another tragic move on the part of Vogue at this point in time was that according to Jeanne Niswonger in *That Doll Ginny*, (published by the author), Mrs. Graves did not believe in television advertising. This would prove to be a grave error on the part of Vogue Dolls Inc. Mrs. Graves belonged to a world of the past, a world of "yes ma'ms and no sirs," where one did the "right" thing. Americans were enjoying their post war prosperity more and more, and the resulting leisure time was being filled by television. By 1961, virtually every home in America either personally had a television set, or had access to one through relatives and friends. Children were often plopped in front of the TV, as parents enjoyed the free time given to them by the "electronic babysitter."

Mrs. Graves obviously felt that choosing a toy was the parent's responsibility and not the child's. *Ginny*, in fact, had been endorsed by *Parents* magazine, a highly touted "Dr. Spock" type of publication that told depression-born parents all they should be doing to raise the "perfect" child. Mrs. Graves had aimed virtually all her advertising at parents — not children. This was a tactical maneuver that proved the most destructive to the company. Another company would not make that mistake.

Mattel, virtually unknown in the 1950s, introduced *Barbie®* at Toy Fair, 1959. Similiar to Vogue's *Jill*, she was a doll that would turn into an American icon. *Barbie®* was not well recieved by the buyers or the public, but

156.

156. In the early 1960s *Ginny*'s head became vinyl. The body was the walker body from 1957. The decline in quality is evident in the shapeless hair style and simple clothes. Collectors usually want these dolls only to add continuity to their collections. *Ann Tardie collection.*

undaunted, Mattel devised a public relations blitz that bombarded Saturday morning television with commercial after commercial about a "teenage fashion model." Through *Barbie®*, little and not so little girls were playing in the future, looking ahead and learning the skills necessary to be glamorous. More than any generation before, this group of pre-adolescents was being shown that teenage years were the ultimate experience in life. It would be another 20 years before Linda Evans and Joan Collins would show the world that over 40 was the "in" place to be!

All of this attention to teenage sophistication really took a toll on the image of *Ginny*. In 1961, *Jeff*, *Jan* and the hard plastic *Jill* were discontinued. In 1962, *Ginny* had only 15 new outfits, none of them very exciting. Finally, in 1963, a vinyl head with rooted hair was added to *Ginny*. She was marked on the back "GINNY, VOGUE DOLLS, INC., PAT NO. 2687594, Made in U.S.A.", and again had 15 simple outfits designed for her. 1964 saw only 13 new outfits. *Ginny* was slowly being phased out. Vogue had gone into the manufacturing of baby dolls, and was having a moderate success. The company had found its new direction, but *Ginny* was not a part of it.

157. Two "transitional" *Ginnys* from 1964 with vinyl heads sit at the table and chairs made by Vogue a few years earlier. The costumes are just simple cotton dresses. *Author's collection.*

157.

1965 saw *Ginny* as an all vinyl doll marked "GINNY" on her head, and "GINNY, VOGUE DOLLS, INC." on her back. She came dressed in a few little girl costumes, five "Fairytale Land," and nine "Far-Away Lands" styles. Surprisingly, this all vinyl *Ginny* has withstood the test of time, and is a lovely little doll. She had a look of innocence to her, childhood, and laughter that the dolls had not had for years. Interestingly, 19 years later, the new Vogue *Ginnys* would be modeled after this doll, as this would be the doll a new generation of mothers would remember. Collectors are discovering more and more the desirability of the "Made in USA" vinyl *Ginny* dolls.

Also in 1965, a series of vinyl *Jill* was introduced as a special "History Land Series." Herein lie the inconsistencies in collecting! The "Gibson Girl" *Jill* from this series is so rare, that this author has only seen one example in ten years of dealing in dolls, while the Madame Alexander version turns up quite often. Truly the laws of supply and demand are working here, for the Vogue version is just as lovely, yet brings one-eighth the price.

By 1966, the "Made in U.S.A." vinyl *Ginny* had attracted some attention and the line was expanded. Some old series were rejuvenated, such as "Fairytale Land" and "Far-Away Lands," to include some gorgeous pairs of dolls, and a *Ginny Nun* was again available. Even the "regular" costumes for *Ginny* seemed a bit better this year, and included some party dresses and play clothes that were fresh and imaginative.

By 1968, (a period often overlooked by collectors), *Ginny* had nine regular costumes and 24 from the "Far-Away Lands Series," and special dolls such as the *Nun, Nurse, Bride, Cowgirl, Pilgrim,* and *Stewardess* constitute some of the rarest dolls by Vogue. Collectors should be aware that many late 1960s dolls have not yet reached the collectors circuit because the owners have been too busy with schooling, jobs, and entertainment to clean out their old toys. As this generation reaches the age to go out on their own, more of their playthings will surface on the collector's market as they go through their things preparing to move out on their own.

1969 was the last year for the American-made *Ginnys*. She had only ten costumes for

158.

158. By 1966, the "Made in USA" all vinyl *Ginny* did have some imaginative designs. These dolls will eventually be very collectible. *Wee Willie Winkie,* shown here, is a little boy complete with lantern and wrist tag. *Author's collection.*

everyday, and 12 in the "Far-Away Lands Series," attesting to the fact that the public was more interested in *Barbie*®, dressed in fishnet stockings and go-go boots, than in a toddler doll. Unlike today with massive chain stores controlling the market, most toy outlets were owned by independents, and old stock would sit on shelves for years. As late as the mid 1970s it was possible to buy up old stock *Ginnys* from the 1960s, and because of the large number produced, it seemed that *Ginny* never left the marketplace. The 1960s were over, and so, it seemed, was *Ginny!*

159. A late 1960s little girl *Ginny* in her original box. It is very difficult to find these dolls mint-in-box. *Ann Tardie collection.*

159.

160.

160. A group of all-vinyl "Made in USA" *Ginny* dolls. All were bought mint-in-box except the little girl, top center, with blonde braids and original dress. She was so filthy the color of her hair was unrecognizable! Restored according to directions given in the text, one could not tell the difference now. *Author's collection.*

161. 1960s "Made in USA" "Far-Away Lands" *Ginny,* from Spain, in the original box. *Ann Tardie collection.*

161.

The tag reads:

102

Mary Had
A Little Lamb

Created by
VOGUE DOLLS MALDEN
INCORPORATED MASS.

162.

162. 1966 #102 *Mary Lamb*. These "Made in USA" styles had a charm all their own, and are the relatives of the current line of Vogue *Ginnys*. *Ann Tardie collection.*

163. 1969 #522 *Bride*. As pretty as any *Ginny* ever made, this dress is made of the finest heavy slipper satin. The flower cascade is original. (Original price is $7 on her tag!) *Author's collection.*

163.

164.

164. Many experiments were tried in the 1960s. This gorgeous 18in (45.7cm) *Indian* is unmarked. Her clothes are labeled, however, and she is a copy of the little Indian girl from c1965. The larger doll's wrists tag says, "Miss Ginny." No mention of this doll is in the catalog, and she is most unusual. *Author's collection.*

165. Shown with a 1959 *Eskimo* for comparison, this 12in (30.5cm). *Miss Ginny* is also dressed for the North. Her face is identical to the larger *Miss Ginny.* She is marked "Vogue" on her head; clothing is labeled. *Author's collection.*

166. Unusual packaging adds to the mystery of collecting *Ginny* dolls. These dolls from the late 1960s are from the same series and are in two different types of packaging. The doll on the right is a transitional doll, possibly made in Hong Kong. *Author's collection.*

165.

166.

VIII...The 1970s —
The Story Continues!

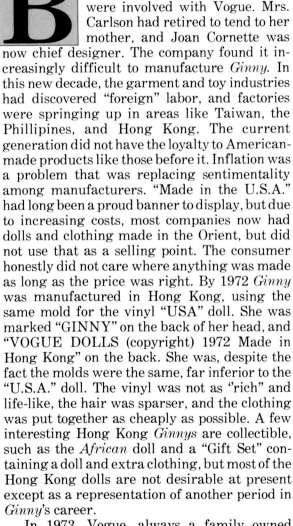

By the 1970s, the Graves family and Virginia Carlson no longer were involved with Vogue. Mrs. Carlson had retired to tend to her mother, and Joan Cornette was now chief designer. The company found it increasingly difficult to manufacture *Ginny*. In this new decade, the garment and toy industries had discovered "foreign" labor, and factories were springing up in areas like Taiwan, the Phillipines, and Hong Kong. The current generation did not have the loyalty to American-made products like those before it. Inflation was a problem that was replacing sentimentality among manufacturers. "Made in the U.S.A." had long been a proud banner to display, but due to increasing costs, most companies now had dolls and clothing made in the Orient, but did not use that as a selling point. The consumer honestly did not care where anything was made as long as the price was right. By 1972 *Ginny* was manufactured in Hong Kong, using the same mold for the vinyl "USA" doll. She was marked "GINNY" on the back of her head, and "VOGUE DOLLS (copyright) 1972 Made in Hong Kong" on the back. She was, despite the fact the molds were the same, far inferior to the "U.S.A." doll. The vinyl was not as "rich" and life-like, the hair was sparser, and the clothing was put together as cheaply as possible. A few interesting Hong Kong *Ginnys* are collectible, such as the *African* doll and a "Gift Set" containing a doll and extra clothing, but most of the Hong Kong dolls are not desirable at present except as a representation of another period in *Ginny's* career.

In 1973, Vogue, always a family owned business, was sold to the Tonka Corporation. Interested in the name "Vogue" as having some meaning in the doll world, the company continued the Melrose, Massachusetts plant. By 1975 *Ginny* was not the big mainstay of the company. Dolls, such as *Miss Ginny*, 15in (38.1cm) dressed in "mod" clothing, were floating

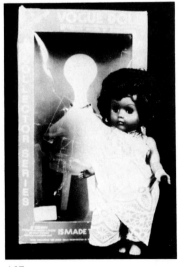

167.

167. 1972 #1802, *Africa*. Considered by most collectors to be the only real valuable doll of the Hong Kong period. *Ann Tardie collection.*

along on the names "Vogue" and "*Ginny*," but it is doubtful that Mrs. Graves herself could have picked this doll out of a lineup to be a *Ginny* doll.

By 1976, the "Far-Away Lands Series" was all that was left. *Ginny* as a little girl had ceased to be desirable, and the foreign costumed series was basically offered as a low cost alternative to the foreign costumed dolls made by Madame Alexander. Once *Ginny* and *Wendy* could stand side by side, each holding their own. Now, these former shadows of *Ginny* looked ludicrous next to the high quality Madame Alexander dolls of the period.

In 1977, Vogue Dolls Inc. became a subsidiary of Lesney Products, and moved the entire operation to Moonachie, New Jersey. Lesney, that first year, continued the "Far-Away Lands" dolls, and used a new mold for another series with painted eyes that included an American Pioneer Girl. This doll is lovely, and was a refreshing new change in *Ginny*'s history.

The biggest surprise to collectors, however, came at Toy Fair in 1978. Lesney, whom one remembers for their "Matchbox" cars, had decided to rejuvenate *Ginny*. At Toy Fair, in New York, a media blitz announced in proud headlines that "Ginny is back!". The advertising was definitely aimed at the mother of the little girl who once owned *Ginny* herself. The company wanted this new generation of children to love and cherish the same doll as their mother did. Ads showed 1950s children holding *Ginny* dolls, (carefully chosen not to look too good, thus upstaging the new dolls), while a new generation of children was shown with the new *Ginny*. Slightly misleading, the ads gave the impression that *Ginny* had not been available for years... actually since 1951 when "Hi...I'm Ginny" appeared on a doll, stores had never been without *Ginny*.

By 1980-1981, these dolls were given an "upbeat" image by involving a Broadway design house, Sasson, in the creation of *Ginny* fashions. Actually the Sasson fashions were very imaginative, and capitalized on the "Roller Disco" craze, and other trends of the time. These *Ginnys* were not highly successful as would be the dolls of 1984-1985. Interesting social changes in the later 1970s made the timing not right for the Lesney product. Additionally, the Lesney

168.

168. 1972 #1001 "Gift Set." This set is the other collectible of the Hong Kong period. The box says "Vogue Dolls, Melrose, MA 02176. A subsidiary of Tonka Corporation." *Ann Tardie collection.*

Ginnys did not look at all like the previous *Ginny* dolls. Mothers could not make the connection. The name was just not enough to carry a doll that once out of the box, one had to think hard who she was. Unlike the *Ginnys* of today, that are truly the likeness of the "Made in USA" *Ginny*'s of the last generation, the Lesney *Ginnys* were "cute," but not *Ginny*.

In the late 1970s, the baby boomers, that is children born after World War II, were going through a rough time. Denied the "American Dream" they were promised in college in the late 1960s, they were bitter and resentful. Having spent a lifetime acquiring style and sophistication, they were not ready to surrender their youth. Being the largest group in the United States, they didn't have to. Much to the annoyance of those born before and those born after, this age group, now in their late twenties and early thirties, by 1978, were not ready to step down as models, actresses, or anything else for that matter. The word "Yuppie" (Young Urban Professional) came to symbolize an upward mobile young couple, well educated, and well dressed, wearing styles a generation before them would have thought "inappropriate" for people their age.

These women, now mothers of young daughters, saw nothing "sacred" in *Ginny*, in 1978. Many, in fact, resented the roles taught by dolls in general, and the woman's movement, not yet having found itself, created unrest in women who were 30, but neither felt, nor looked "washed up," and refused to settle down to dust curtain rods and serve milk and cookies as their mothers had years before.

In my opinion, society was still trying to find itself, and the timing of the Lesney *Ginnys* was off. Add to that the fact they did not resemble *Ginny*, and it is obvious why they were not highly successful. The 1980's would again make women comfortable with themselves, with most women feeling that a family and a career didn't have to be a choice anymore. America, children, and collectors were ready for a new *Ginny* by 1984!

169.

169. 1977 *Jamaican* and *Colonial Girl*. Made in Hong Kong, but with painted eyes. These are going to be highly collectible as they were made for only one year. *Ann Tardie collection.*

170. *Woman's Day* ad for *Ginny*, 1979. Ads like this for the Lesney *Ginnys* tried to capitalize on nostalgia. By and large, it was not successful. *Author's collection.*

171. *Good Housekeeping* ad, 1979. Lesney's campaign was aimed at mothers who loved *Ginny* themselves. The new dolls, however, did not resemble the old *Ginnys*, and mothers could not relate to it. *Ann Tardie collection.*

170.

171.

172. A valuable Lesney *Ginny* is this *Ginnette*. She is the black version of *Ginny*. It is interesting that the old name was used for this doll. The reason remains a mystery! *Author's collection.*

172.

173. The Lesney furniture was very imaginative and had lots of great accessories. Collectors would do well to buy up remaining stock when available, as these pieces will undoubtedly become valuable. *Ann Tardie collection.*

173.

174. This poster was included in "Ginny's Sweet Shoppe," a play setting for 1979. *Ann Tardie collection.*

175. The moped, made by Lesney, is the hardest to find of the 1978-1979 accessories. It is already bringing double the original price! *Ann Tardie collection.*

174.

175.

The World *Ginny*

OUTFIT NO. 922-
©1978 VOGUE D
MOONACHIE, N
MADE IN HON

176. Catalog houses such as Sears, Penneys, and Montgomery Wards carried the Lesney *Ginnys*. They were shipped in plain white boxes such as this. *Author's collection.*

177. The real "prize" of the Lesney period will be the "Gift Set." Sealed in plastic, most will not survive intact. These were listed in the catalog, but not widely available. *Author's collection.*

177.

178. Lesney *Ginnys* enjoying an evening at home! *Ann Tardie collection.*

179. "Ginny's Sweet Shoppe," from 1979, with a juke box and popcorn machine. *Ann Tardie collection.*

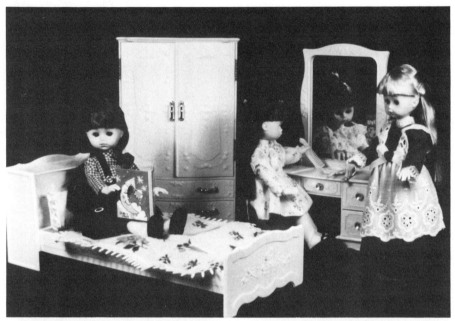

178.

179.

180. The name "Sasson" was supposed to give the Lesney *Ginnys* an identity. While nicely made, they weren't very popular. *Author's collection.*

180.

181. Catalog pages from the 1981 Lesney Catalog. Lesney is no longer in operation, making the dolls from that period future collectibles. As they were made by the millions, they are currently available in some stores. *Author's collection.*

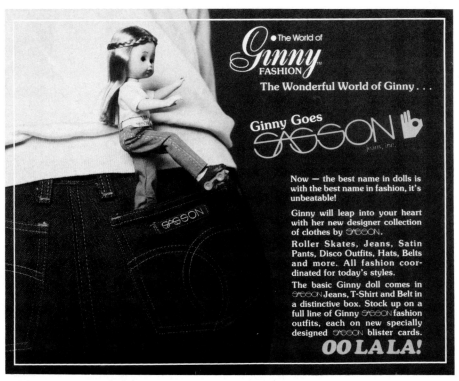

181.

IX...1984 — A New Beginning

As stated previously, the allure of *Ginny* was that she stimulated a child's imagination, and was represented as a strong, sturdy little girl who was afraid of nothing. A child, through *Ginny*, could overcome the fear of such events as a first day at school, by seeing that *Ginny* could survive these traumas and remain unscathed.

In 1983, Lesney's last attempt at *Ginny* dolls was a series of "International Brides." Time will probably pronounce them worthy as collectibles, but they were cheaply made. The Oriental dolls were especially nice, and the series is necessary to a comprehensive *Ginny* collection. Later that year, Lesney ceased to exist as a toy company.

In October 1983, Walter (Wally) Reiling, a man with 30 years of experience in the toy business, secured the rights to both "Ginny" and "Vogue." As president of Meritus Industries, a New Jersey based company, Mr. Reiling is in many ways like Jennie Graves. A forward-thinking man, "Wally" as he is known, views *Ginny* the same way Mrs. Graves did. In 1984, at Toy Fair in New York, Vogue dolls again opened its doors. The new dolls, delightful in every way, truly recaptured the *Ginny* of the late 1960s, and even held their own with the gorgeous strung dolls of the 1950s. In a daring display of courage, Mr. Reiling displayed the new *Ginny* next to a beautiful mint doll from 1952, a move that no other manufacturer would dare risk. The two compare beautifully and each show the skill and craftsmanship of their creator.

New to the 1984 Vogue line are porcelain *Ginny* dolls, making this the first time *Ginny* has been offered in ceramic. The line includes many different hair styles and colors, just like the *Ginny* of old!

In 1985, Vogue, under Mr. Reiling's guidance, introduced *Ginnette*, the baby sister of *Ginny*. Also available in procelain, she is made much the same way *Ginnette* was constructed in the 1950s. A basic boxed doll in panties, shoes and socks, with a whole array of boxed outfits, the 1985 *Ginny* is a collector's dream. Dazzling pairs such as *Bride and Groom, Hansel and*

182.

182. *Ginny* is back! Vogue announced the return of *Ginny* done in the style of the past at Toy Fair, 1984. Children and collectors alike were delighted with the little doll. *Author's collection.*

Gretel and *Jack and Jill* bring back fond memories and will surely be a hit with the 1980s woman, secure in herself, and now ready to have her daughter share in the memory of *Ginny.*

The climax of our story would not be complete without a royal ending...and Vogue has provided just that! The reissue of the *Coronation Queen,* the most luxurious doll of the Golden Era of the 1950s, once again makes *Ginny,* Queen of the 1980s.

To many of us, *Ginny* will always be the epitome of the best of childhood...the promises kept, the dreams realized. We who loved her then, love her now. We hope there will always be a *GINNY!*

183. 1984 *Antique Lace* in red, and *Holiday Girl* in blue. The beautiful fabrics and rich colors made the 1984 dolls a huge success. They were one of the few dolls able to satisfy both collector and child that year. *Ann Tardie collection.*

183.

184. Vogue made this exclusive *Ginny Fairy Godmother* just for Meyers, a store in northern New Jersey that carried *Ginny* right from the beginning. *Ann Tardie collection.*

184.

185. The porcelain *Ginnys* made by Vogue are something new for *Ginny.* Hauntingly like the bisque "Just Me" of the 1920s, these hand-crafted dolls are done in the style of Jennie Graves. *Vogue doll photo.*

186. Vogue, like Lesney, has issued furniture. This charming bed will be a collectible of the future. *Vogue photo.*

185.

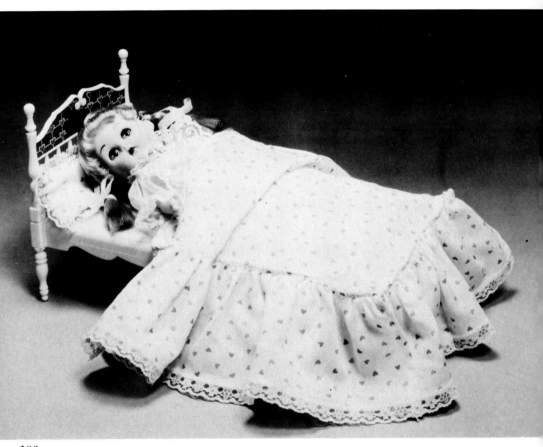

186.

187. New for 1985 is *Ginny's* Pony.
Like *Ginny's* Pup in the 1950s he
has no name! Her pup was called
"Sparky" in a book. We wonder
when her pony will get a name.
Vogue photo.

187.

188. 1985 *Jack and Jill.* The style and fabric used are very much like the 1952 set. We, as collectors, are thrilled by such care to detail. *Vogue photo.*

189. 1985 *Ginnette.* Again, *Ginny's* baby sister is back to delight children and collectors alike. *Vogue photo.*

188.

189.

190.

190 & 191. The basic *Ginny* concept has returned. Her extra boxed clothes are just too pretty to open. *Vogue photo.*

192. 1985 *Coronation Queen.* Once again, *Ginny* takes her place as "Queen of Dolls." Thirty years later, a new generation will love and adore her just as much! *Vogue photo.*

191.

192.

Index